CORK IN THE
1960s

PHOTOGRAPHS BY ANTHONY BARRY

COMPILED BY ORLA & TERRY KELLY
WITH MICHAEL LENIHAN

WITH A FOREWORD BY THEO DORGAN

MERCIER PRESS
Irish Publisher – Irish Story

Dedicated to Rita Barry

MERCIER PRESS
Cork
www.mercierpress.ie

© Orla Kelly, 2014
© Foreword: Theo Dorgan, 2014

ISBN: 978 1 78117 249 0

10 9 8 7 6 5 4 3 2 1

A CIP record for this title is available from the British Library

This book is sold subject to the condition that it shall not, by way of trade or otherwise, be lent, resold, hired out or otherwise circulated without the publisher's prior consent in any form of binding or cover other than that in which it is published and without a similar condition including this condition being imposed on the subsequent purchaser.

No part of this publication may be reproduced or transmitted in any form or by any means, electronic or mechanical, including photocopying, recording or any information or retrieval system, without the prior permission of the publisher in writing.

Printed and bound in the EU.

FOREWORD

THEO DORGAN

What it is about photographs that can shake the foundations of the present moment so thoroughly? This is the city of my childhood, where light, poverty, voices and rain flickered through all-too-solid streets, where people seemed dense and solid, too, in ways that would fade away over the years until most of what I remember seems to me now no more substantial than ... a photograph, an image snatched in light from the flow of darkness.

I remember the cityscape Barry has captured here, but I remember more rain; I remember the texture of walls, the depths of doorways, the smell of rotting fruit and old clothes on the Coal Quay, pipes in the mouths of men – I remember the same things he sees and pictures here, and I remember things very differently, too. We are expected to agree that, at a given time, a place is the same place for everyone. Well, yes and no. These photographs have me saying, yes I remember this and that, just as he pictures it, but also resisting, saying no, there was something else, too – or perhaps I imagined it, have been nurturing a false memory all these years. This is the confounding thing about photographs like these – they confirm and at the same time undermine our faith in memory.

Here are some things that strike me from Anthony Barry's flow of images: how much the city is changed, how hard and suspicious are the faces of those who sense themselves being photographed, how often the photographer's eye is drawn to men and women deep in conversation, how many of the men are wearing hats and caps, how almost all the women are wearing hats or headscarves, how often the clothes seem home-made, especially on children, how little the city has changed ...

And here are some things that seem mysteriously absent: joyful faces, the river, trees and parks, benches, interiors, children at play, hurling matches, priests, soldiers, flags ...

I scan backwards and forwards through these photographs, torn between recognition and doubt: I was a child in this city, learning the map of it on my pulses while Anthony Barry was walking the streets, methodically recording people and places – his city maps onto mine, but it is not the same city, then or now.

Some of this has mechanical explanation: I was a child, looking up all the time, up at faces, bodies, buildings, while Barry (and this is striking, somehow) very often favoured the downward-looking vantage point, or at least was on level terms, so to speak, with his subjects.

Point of view matters. I was learning this city, he was appropriating a place he already knew.

I imagine him muttering to himself as he walked the streets, talking to himself about this shot or that, telling himself when to shoot and when not to shoot, chatting quietly to himself about f-stops, apertures, perspective ... and then in the alchemy of printing deciding what to keep, what to isolate, what to let go. And I imagine – no,

I remember – the child I was on the same streets, the never-ending dialogue ... look at the scarf on that woman, like Mam's ... who's that talking to the busman, I know him to see ... Suzuki, thought it was a Honda ... mind those lads outside the Munster Arcade, they'd bump you off the footpath ... woman reading books, wonder what books ... on and on and on. Building the world.

And now these photographs, still moments snatched out of time, out of the city's overlay of talk over talk; so many men and women and children, some still among the living, some long since gone to the shades; cars that are rusting in landfill, shops, quays and offices that are still standing, that have been transformed, re-made, demolished – and the stories, the thousands of stories on which these photographs touch: did that relaxed garda get off with the obviously interested young woman? Who was that cool dude in the shades, with the lawnmower in the boot of his Mercedes outside the Château? What was he up to? And all those conversations, where did they find the time for so much talk?

And that is perhaps what I love most about this book – what it snatches from the dissolving acids of time, certainly, but more than that, what it confirms for those of us who remember, what it offers as prompts to thought for those who come to these photographs as pointers to an unknown city that is somehow also a known and familiar place.

Let one image snatched from the flow stand for all: Mamie Murphy on Camden Quay. I remember her golden smile, her shawled, queenly presence. I remember her oranges, each in its rustling fragrant nest of blue tissue paper. My father stopping the bicycle after the rush of our swift descent down Roman Street, Mulgrave Road, me hopping off the crossbar to buy us two oranges for the match, the way she'd pat my hand as she handed back the change, smile over my head at my smiling father. Anthony Barry has caught her perfectly. What an eye he had!

INTRODUCTION

ORLA KELLY

Anthony Barry will be best known to Cork people for his famous blend of Barry's Tea, which he created and sold in his shop in Prince's Street in Cork. He will also be known for his political contribution to Cork, serving in the Dáil and Seanad Éireann and also as Lord Mayor of Cork from 1961 to 1962.

What may surprise some is his artistic vocation, which he pursued throughout his career in both tea blending and politics. Anthony Barry was consumed with the art of photography and never left the house without either his Leica or Rolleiflex camera round his neck. His mission was to record the architecture and people of Cork city. Every day, as he walked from his home in York Terrace (where he lived from 1944) to the tea shop in Prince's Street, he would photograph Cork citizens going about their daily business: the commercial and social aspects of the city, but also all the labour of the city, from the ships on the quayside to the shawlies trading on the Coal Quay. His aim was to capture his subjects unaware, thus recording the true goings-on of a city, whether it be the idle musings of those waiting in a bus queue or the smartly turned out family on a trip into the city.

Anthony Barry approached his photography as an art and constantly strove for interesting compositions and images with high contrast light and shadow. An innate eye for taking his subjects unawares makes his photographs even more compelling. Such technical skills allow the architecture of the streets to become more sharply defined and reveal people's facial expressions clearly. The family bath at home in York Terrace was often commandeered for developing photographs for hours at a time and family members were warned to use the bathroom beforehand. Another room was taken over for a darkroom and that too was off limits to all. He had experimented with sepia tinting his photographs as early as the fifties and was an avid reader of photographic journals and *National Geographic* magazine. Unlike current digital images, there was much labour involved in producing a photographic print and thus only the best images made it to a full-sized print. Barry always worked in black and white and each photograph was meticulously labelled and mounted in an album. It is from this astounding collection of 7,500 images that the photographs for this book were chosen.

The focus for this sequel to *No Lovelier City* (1995) is the citizens of Cork during the 1960s. It highlights the transition from one era to the next and the imminent changes are apparent in how people dress and in the streets they inhabit. With so few cars on the streets, Cork is a more intimate city – everyone appears to have time to stop and talk at their leisure. One senses the sea change that is occurring as one generation of women, who are traditionally hatted or headscarved, pass the next generation of women who sport beehive haircuts, mini dresses and knee-high boots. It is as though a generation was skipped. These younger women are more influenced by London fashion than their parents, yet both walk with the Corkonian's sense of pride.

Portrait of Anthony Barry reading *Corriere della Sera*. Barry travelled often in Europe and North Africa and took many photographs on his travels. His son John left Cork to join the Christian Brothers in Italy at the age of eighteen and Anthony kept a close eye on Italian politics and current affairs.

Although Barry had collected and recorded this wonderfully comprehensive view of life in Cork city during this time, his photographs were never published or exhibited in his lifetime. It is now that they take on a new significance as they reveal a wealth of social and architectural history. We only realise that boys in short pants, nuns in wimples and families in handmade clothes are missing when we are reminded by these images that they once existed. It is a very comprehensive record of the city and her inhabitants and this was clearly Barry's focus as the more traditional sea or landscape image failed to seduce him. Even when he travelled abroad, it was the city streets of London or Rome that drew him in and in Africa the mysterious faces of traders in the narrow alleyways of the souks which made for the kind of composition he loved.

As his granddaughter I remember always being photographed, as were all the family. The difference on this occasion is that he would be much more intrigued by the silhouette of a first haircut or a child staring into a rock pool in Garretstown than other more formal occasions. When he took portraits it was with the eye and aspirations of a painter: composition, depth of field, light and shadow were all paramount and we were all accustomed to being patient during this process. We are now all rewarded with an extraordinary collection of family photographs.

There is a subtle similarity between the art of tea blending and that of photography. Each begin with some ingredients and the end result must be imagined before it can be created. The slow blending of potions and the patience of delicate infusions are undertaken in a studied silence. The sum is greater than the parts and a slow and meticulous process reveals a strong and distinct result. It is no coincidence that Anthony Barry chose these two quite different avenues to pursue his artistic talents. Fortunately we can still enjoy both of them today.

Fruit boxes from Brazil and tea chests from Ceylon make a sharp contrast to Corkonians looking for bargains in Punch's on Cornmarket Street, commonly known as the Coal Quay. The woman on the right of Portney's Lane, wearing the checked cardigan, is May Duggan, a Coal Quay dealer.

Children on Lavitt's Quay play an animated game on a riverbank bench. In the background are some classic cars, such as a Ford Anglia, a Wolseley and a Fiat 850.

Boys fishing, a favourite pastime for Corkonians young and old alike, at O'Donovan's Bridge by the Gaol Cross entrance to University College Cork.

A family stops for a chat on the Grand Parade, wearing the fashions of the day: boys in short pants and anoraks, and the girl to the left wearing a trendy coat and shoes. There is no shortage of signage on the street, which includes Avis car hire and R. J. Curtis, chemist, at No. 43.

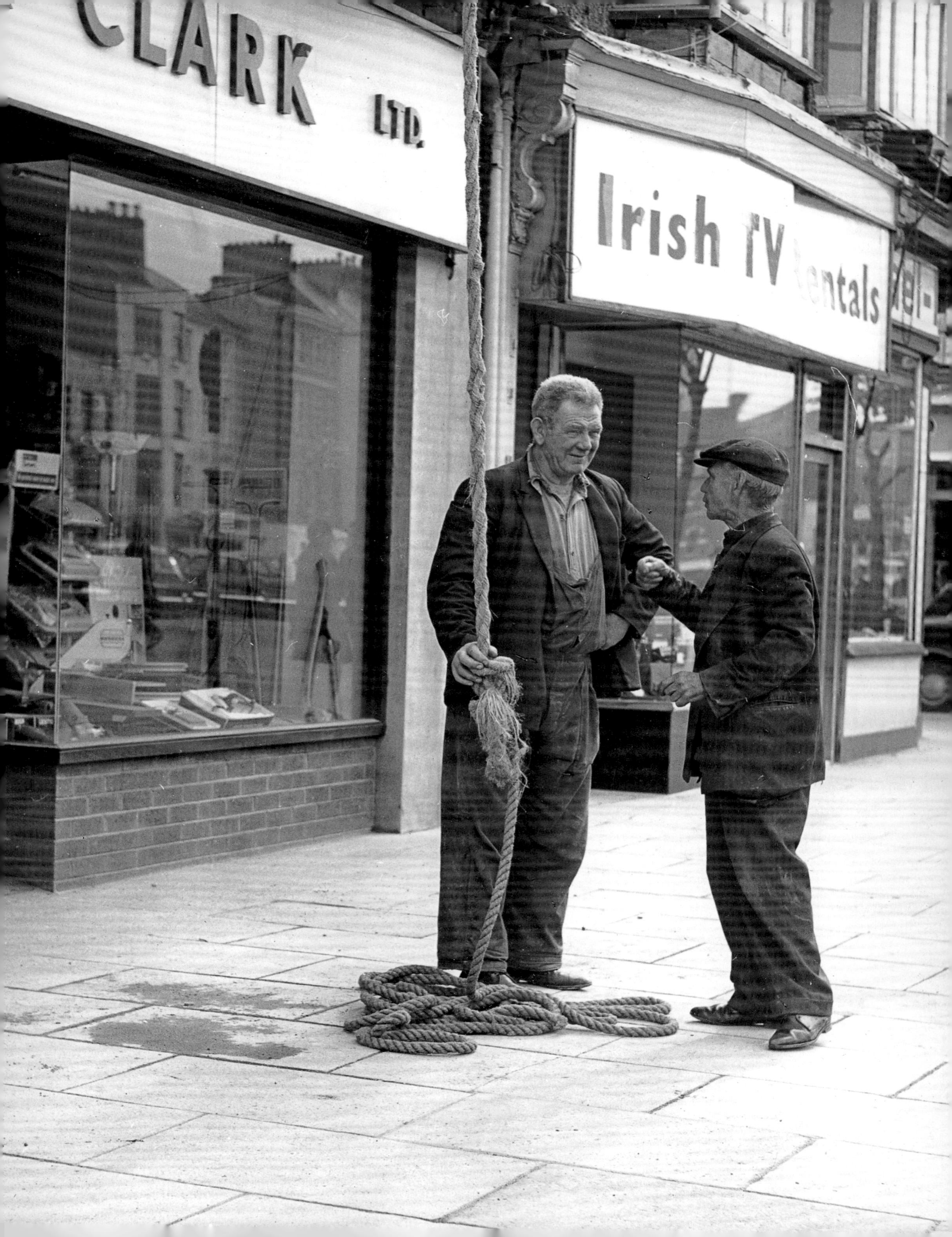
CLARK
LTD.
Irish TV Rentals

Above: The *Irish Independent* office at 35 Patrick's Street when the *Cork Examiner* had competition from its Dublin rivals. A poster for the *Sunday Independent* focuses on the birth control debate, a hot topic in 1960s Ireland following the marketing of the pill, and sport and wedding photographs adorn the window. Outside, the chrome-plated Silver Cross pram was the essence of comfort for small babies.

Left: Even this man working outside Frank Clark's hardware shop on the Parade had time to stop and chat. Irish TV Rentals were renting out the latest in black and white televisions.

People crossing the North Mall at the bottom of Shandon Street, at a time when traffic was light and it was a safer prospect. The temporary Bailey bridge in the background was a feature of the cityscape for many years, even after the new Griffith Bridge, which replaced the old North Gate Bridge, was completed.

A man standing near the Old Kentucky Restaurant in North Main Street leans against a hand-painted sign for wellingtons and boots. The takeaway menu advertises barbecued chickens, Kentucky burgers, sausages, chips and ice cream cones.

Above: Kilgrew's toy shop, on the corner of North Main Street and Kyle Street. Clothes are being sold from the pavement on Kyle Street and in the background, on the right, an old Thames van can be seen.

Right: On Patrick's Street a man smoking a cigarette, with his suitcase at his feet, is waiting for a bus as people walk by. Four CIÉ bus stops were located on this busy section of Patrick's Street. The No. 7a to Montenotte has just stopped to take on passengers.

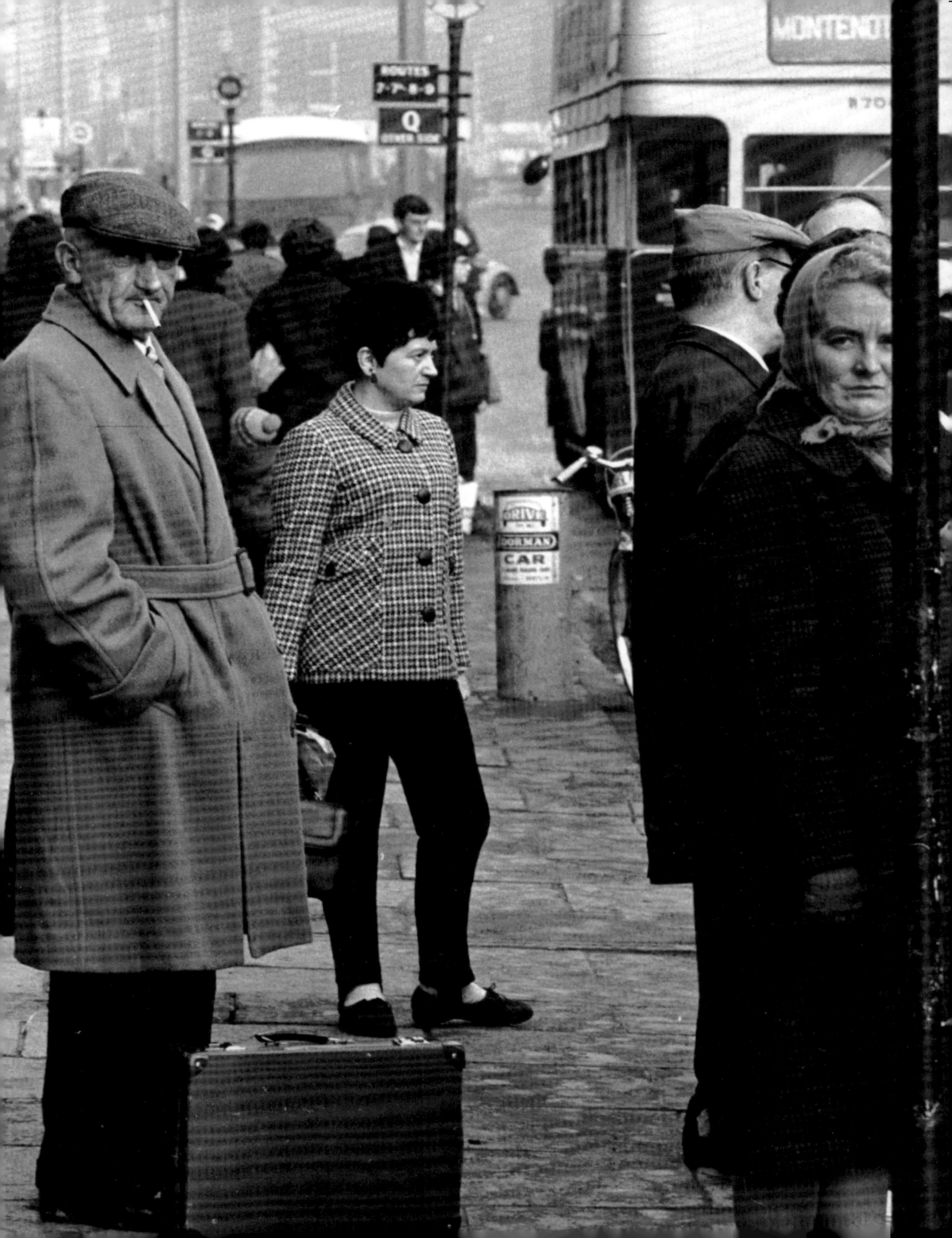
MONTENOT
ROUTES
Q
DRIVE
DORMAN
CAR

Roches Stores, now Debenhams, was one of Cork's most popular shops. The window display at the corner of Maylor Street shows the very latest in ladies' fashion. Roches had been rebuilt in 1927, following the burning of Cork city by members of the crown forces in December 1920.

A woman walks, oblivious to any possible traffic, down a less frenetic Patrick's Street. In the background is Cash's (now Brown Thomas), a shop well known for its fabulous window displays.

Rose O'Keeffe and her son Declan, December 1967. Sound asleep, Declan is totally unaware that Santa's grotto is on the ground floor of Cash's. This department store always had one of the best window displays in the city, particularly at Christmas.

Byrne's butchers, North Main Street, were in direct competition with their neighbour, Murphy's family butchers, and a fine selection of bacon, hams, loin and sausages could be purchased there. Byrne's motto was 'Be on the pig's back with us'.

Above: Bolger's store at 74–75 Patrick's Street was well known as a ladies' and gentlemen's outfitter. It first opened its doors to the Cork public in 1937.

Right: A friendly conversation on the South Mall with a garda. The Edinburgh Assurance Co. and Royal Insurance Co. are in the background of this image. The South Mall was the commercial heart of the city – home to banks, stockbrokers, auctioneers, members of the legal profession and insurance companies. Parked beside the tree is an Austin Maxi.

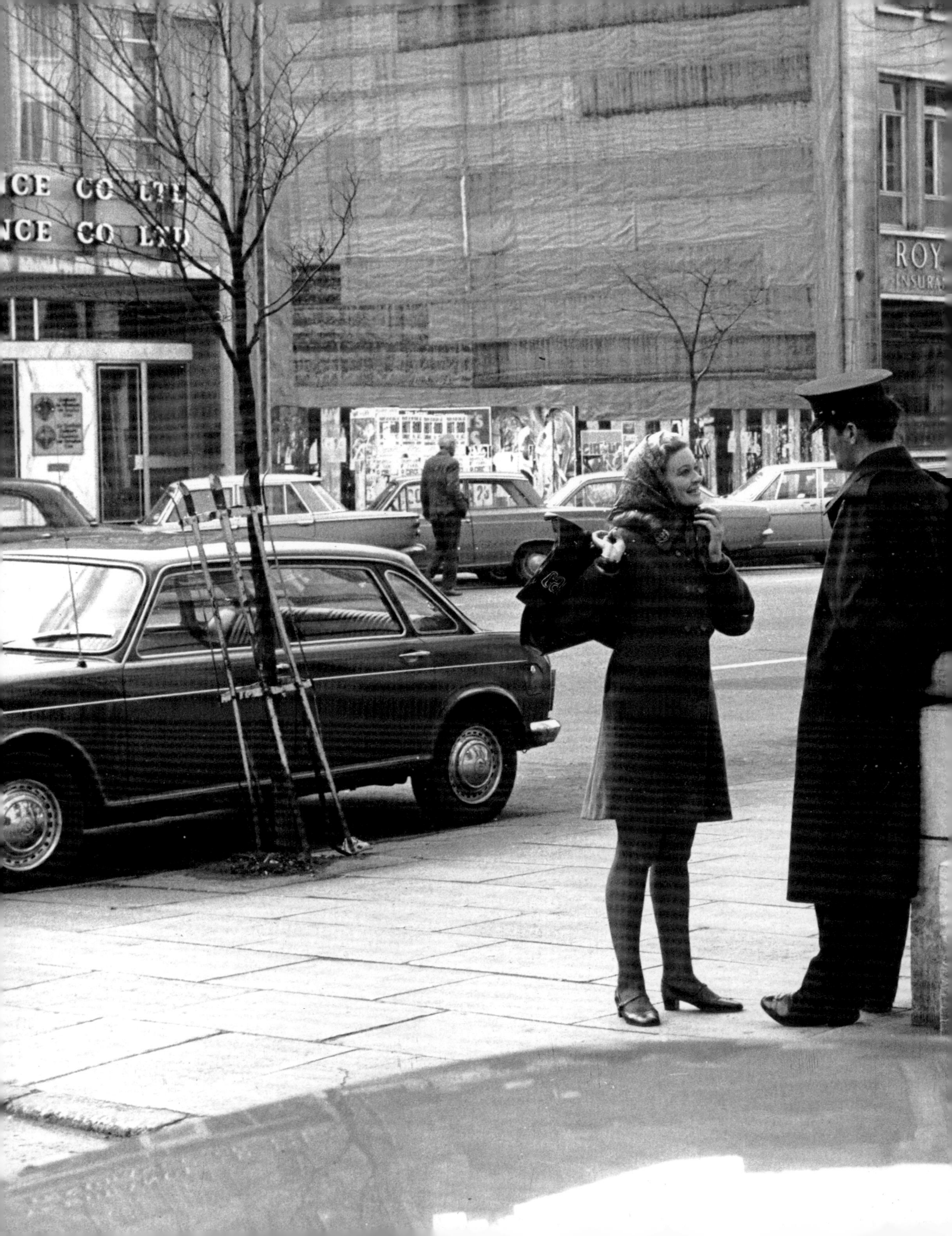
NCE CO LTD
ROY

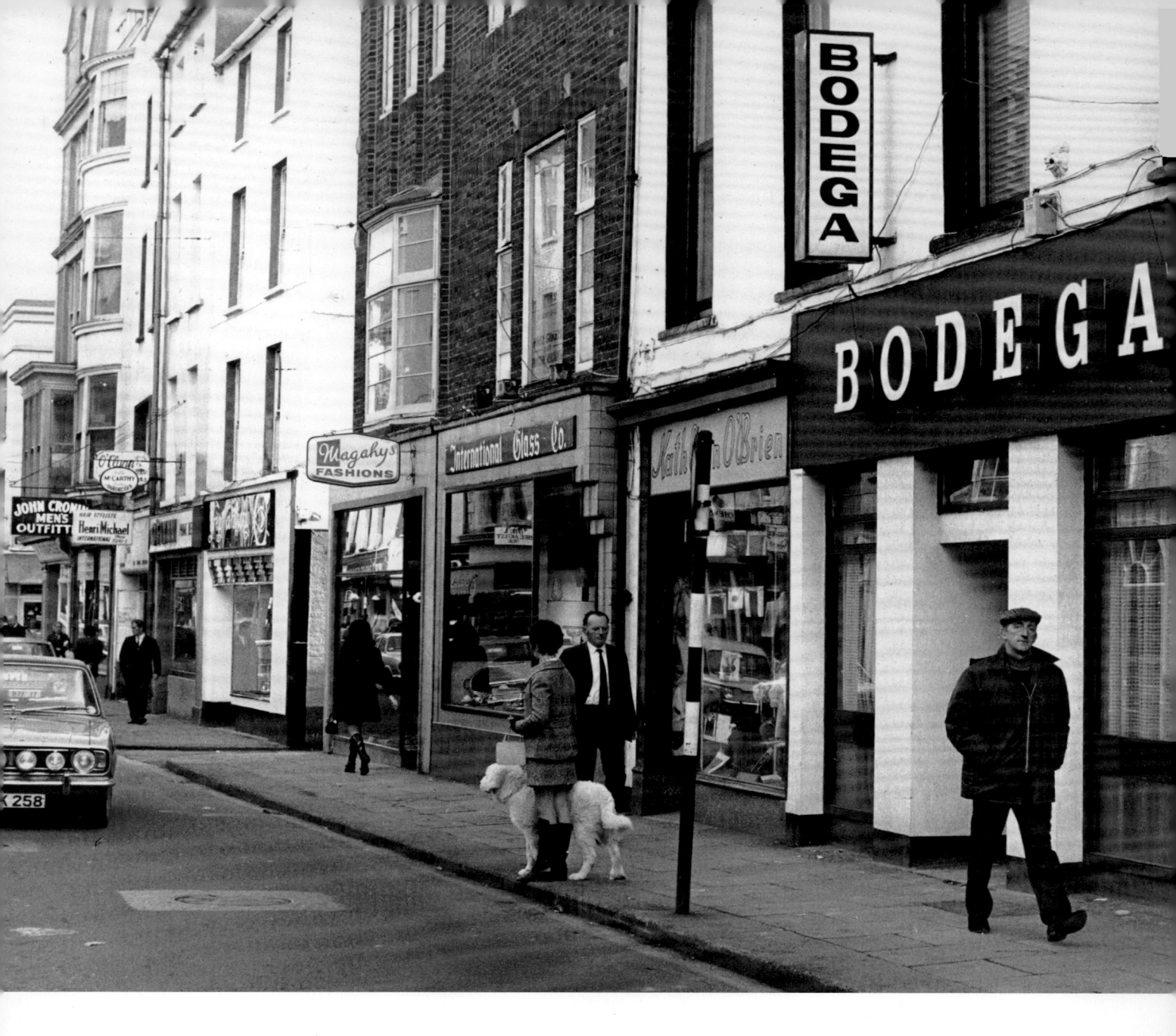

Above: A Ford Cortina Mark II complete with spot lamps makes its way towards the Bodega, a well-known Cork pub on Oliver Plunkett Street. This Bodega may be gone, but the name lives on today on a bar in Cornmarket Street.

Right: Two boys with bags laden with timber take a rest on their way down St Paul's Avenue. This was a common sight when open fires were the main form of heating in nearly every house. To the left over the wall is St Paul's church, which was then being used by the printing firm of Guy & Co.

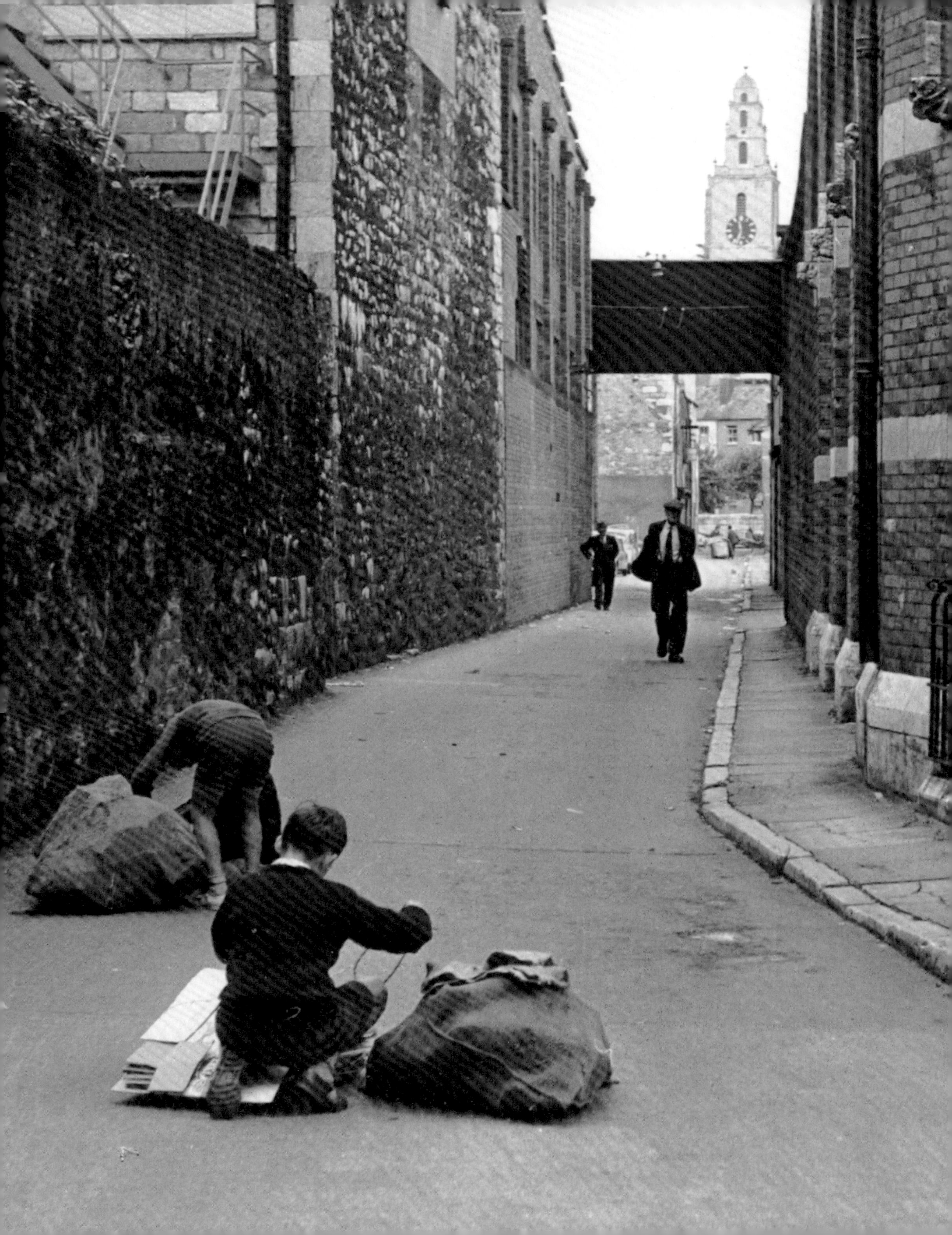

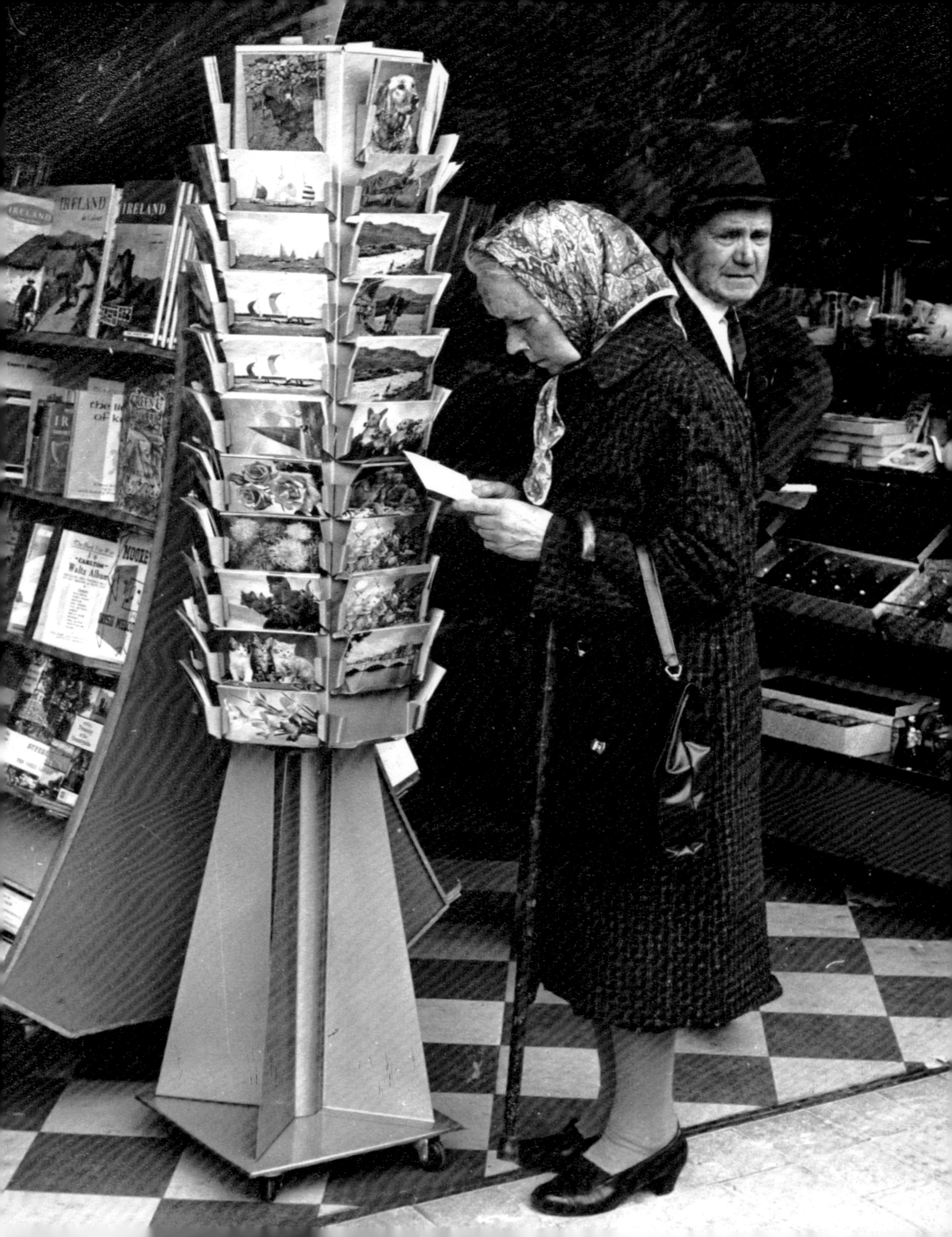
IRELAND
IRELAND
IRELAND
"CARLTON"
Waltz Album

Above: A man reads his paper amongst stacks of timber with Sutton's office in the background. Sutton's, Cork's largest distributor of coal, employed over 250 people before a fire on 29 November 1963 destroyed the premises on the South Mall.

Left: An abundance of cards can be seen on this revolving stand at the old open-fronted Eason's on Patrick's Street, as a lady contemplates whether the postcard she has chosen is suitable.

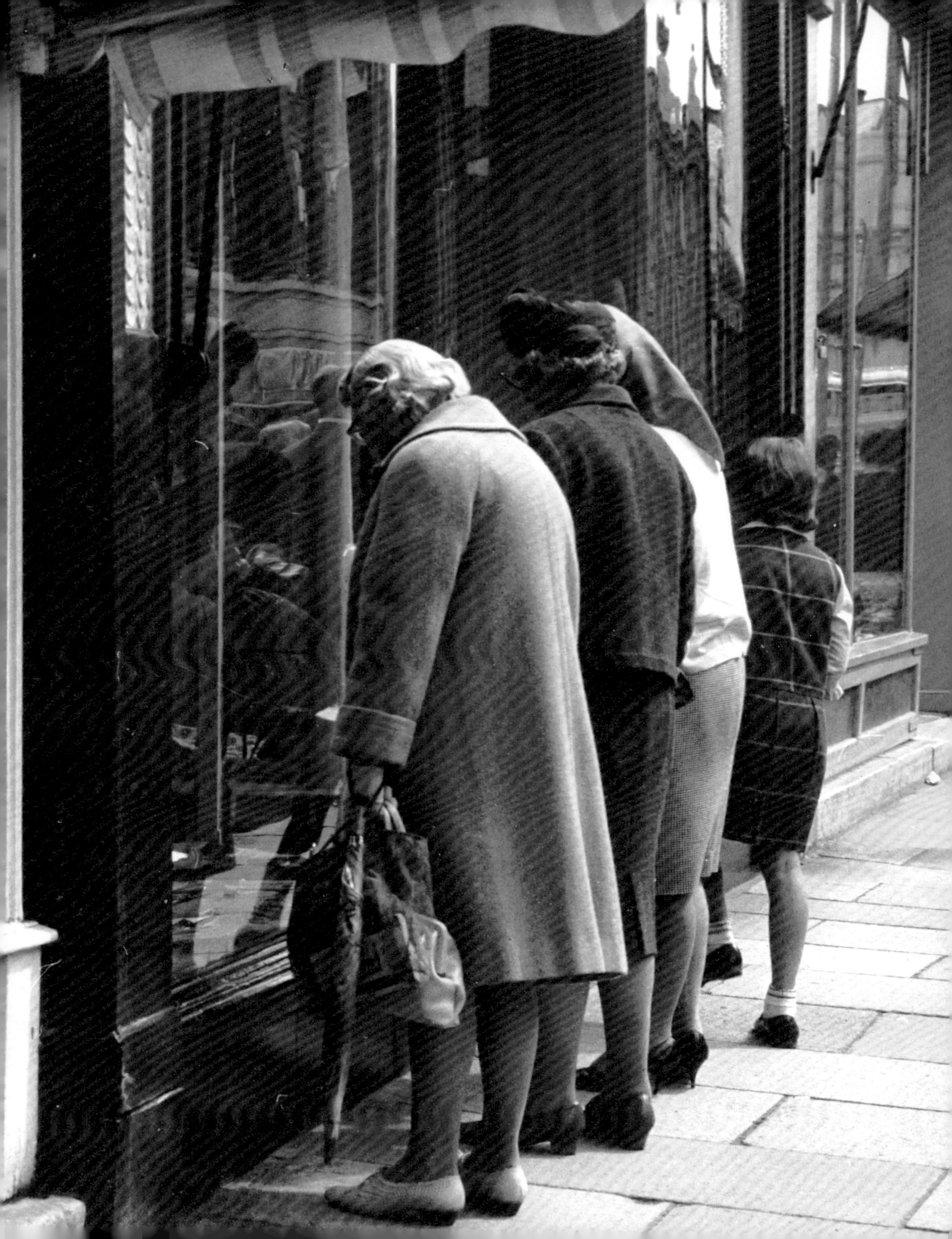

Above: In an era when people had less money, families were still impeccably turned out, as this family on Patrick's Street shows. The sign on the bin advertises motor and scooter parts and after-sales services at the Hanover Cycle Co.

Left: Window-shopping was a favourite Cork occupation, and these ladies seem very interested in the goods displayed.

SALON
ERS COMPANY
MANGAN
M. Atkins
MELINA
HAIRSTYLING
SALON
CROSS
HERE
wine and coffee lounge
TIVOLI GRILL
MANGAN
Chemist
J. BLAIR
Celefon
VZB
327

Above: Girls waiting to collect their boxes for a flag day outside a Cork Caravan Co. horse-drawn caravan. These caravans were a familiar sight in Cork during the 1960s as they were hired out to visiting tourists. On the left is Kathy Lenihan and to the right is Ann Russell.

Left: The Cork Consumers Gas Co., Mangan's pillar clock and the Tivoli restaurant were all once mainstays of Patrick's Street, of which only the clock survives today. Note the man precariously cleaning the windows above another Cork institution, Mangan's jewellers, established in 1817.

Anthony Barry has been spotted taking this picture from a building above by schoolboys who are wearing short pants despite the winter wool coats that the ladies require.

Sitting reading a paper, eating a cone and examining a toy are just some of the activities at this bus queue. As few people had cars, Corkonians seem to have spent a lot of their time waiting for buses, with baskets full of shopping, in a most patient manner.

Above: Passing near the Munster Arcade, now Penneys, on a busy Patrick's Street, two boys look up in wonder.

Right: Two men having a conversation. Across the street is the Saxone Shoes premises, 43 Patrick's Street, once owned by the British Shoe Corporation. Also in the background (*left*) is another Cork institution, Woolworth's, famous for its selection of sweets, ice cream, roasted peanuts and, of course, toys.

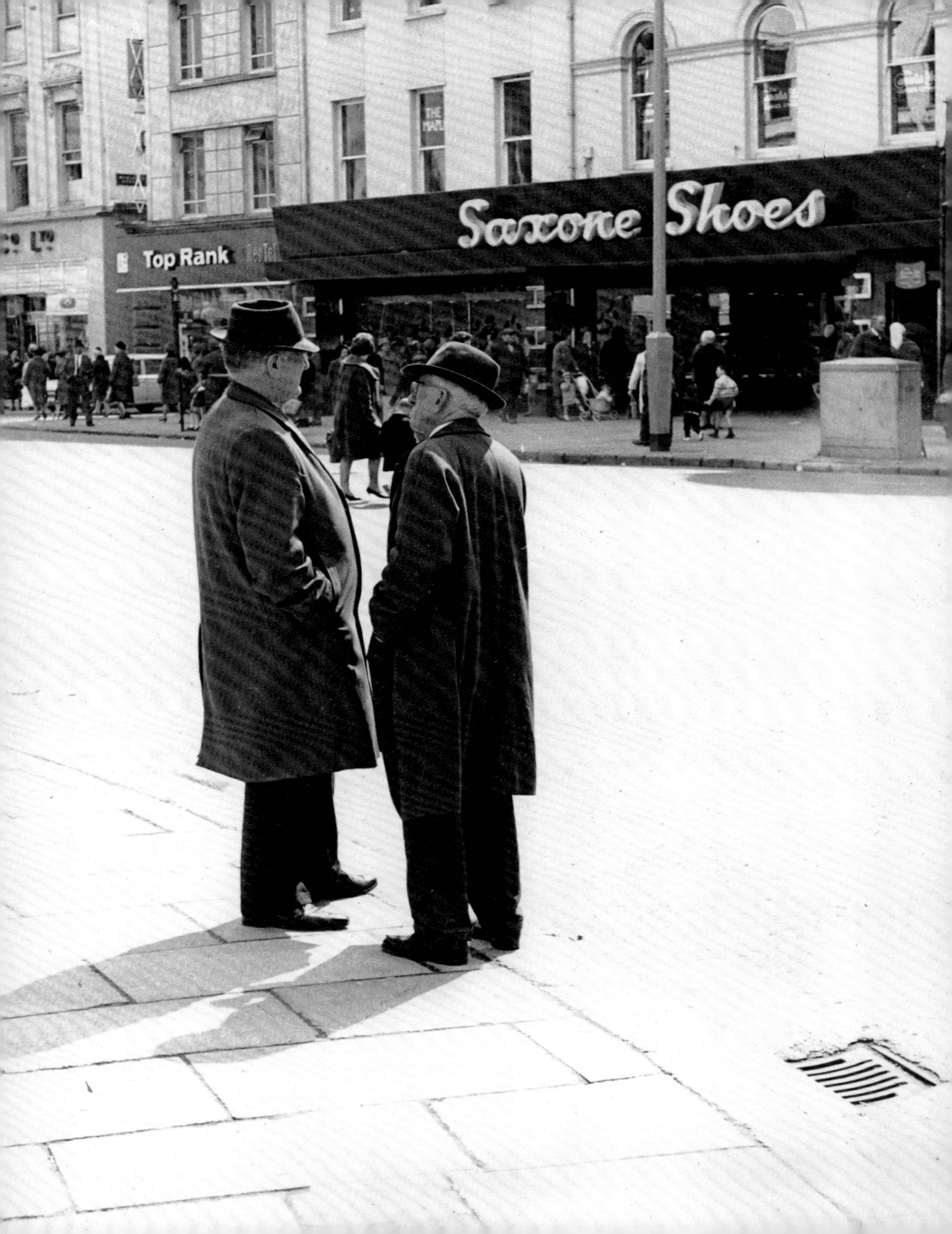
Saxone Shoes
Top Rank

Above: The bus stop outside Saxone Shoes, where waiting for a bus was made easier with a fine display of shoes to peruse. Up overhead the Maple restaurant was well known for its coffees, lunch and grill menu.

Left: This lady is laden down with goods as she stops for a rest outside Jim Galvin's licensed premises on Oliver Plunkett Street.

Above: Opinions are traded outside the entrance to the English Market on Prince's Street.

Overleaf: Another very busy Patrick's Street scene with buses arriving to bring weary shoppers home with their purchases.

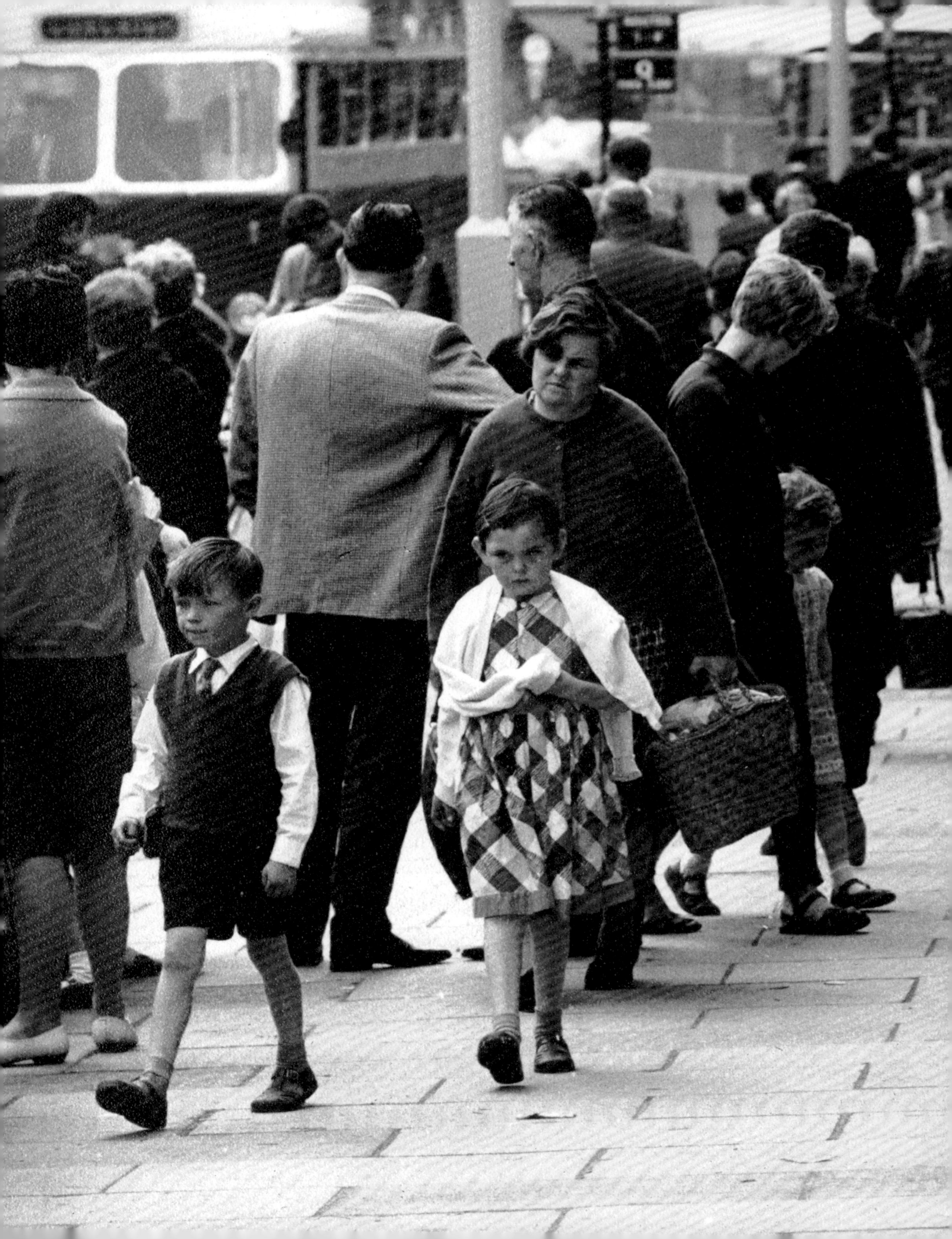

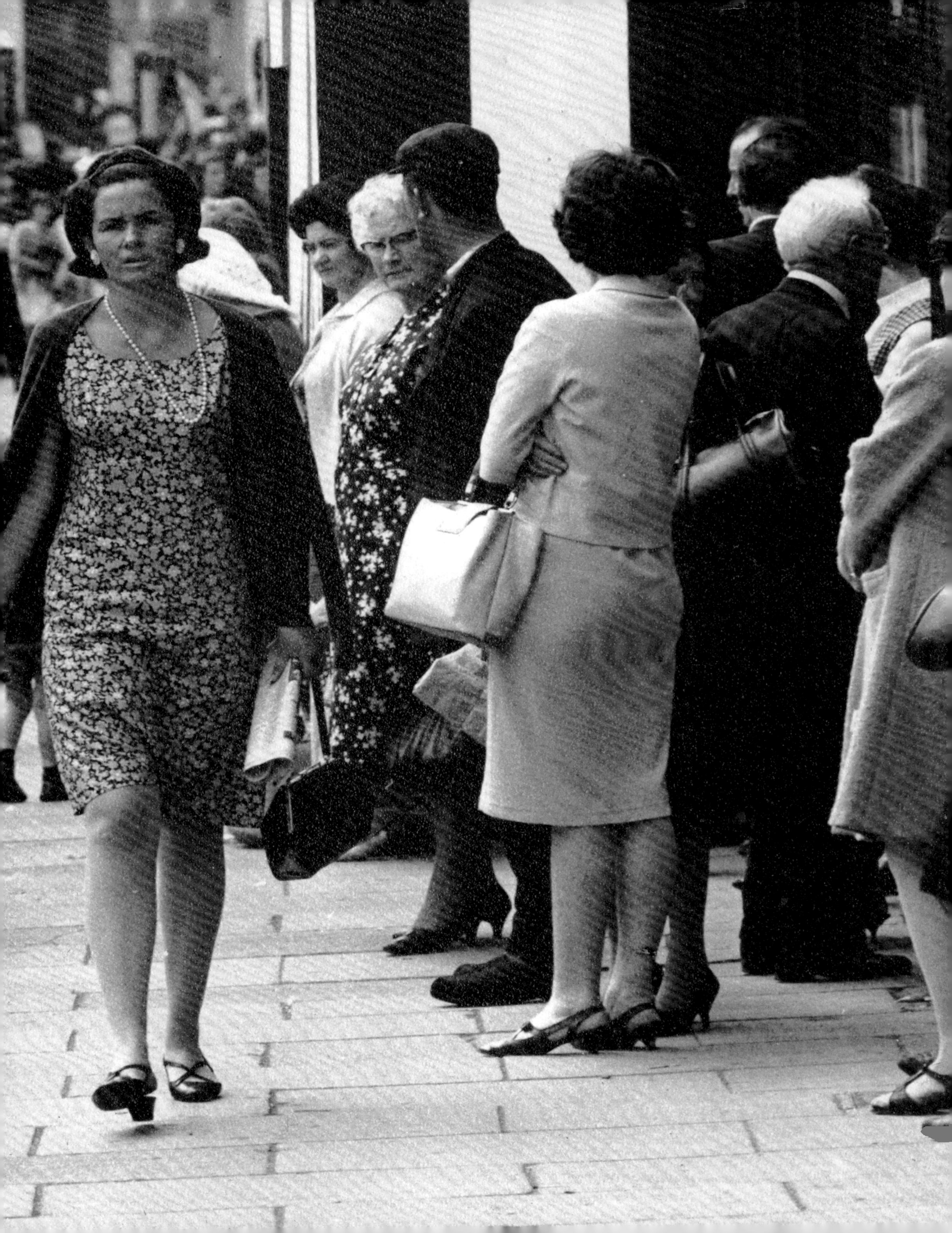

Above: The Coal Quay, where shawlies sold all manner of goods, from prams to mattresses. May Goode, seated in the background, is the dealer.

Right: Two CIÉ busmen hold a conversation as Fr Mathew eavesdrops. 'The Statue', as it is fondly known, has been in place since 10 October 1864, when 100,000 people turned out for its unveiling. In the background are the Old Bridge restaurant and Clancy's Swan & Cygnet pub. The scooters parked by 'The Statue' were a very common form of transport at this time.

FATHER MATHEW
DIED DEC
TH APOSTLE OF TEMPERANCE
A TRIBUTE FROM A GRATEFUL PEOPLE UNVEILED OCT 10TH 1864
OLD BRID
Restaurant
One up one down
NPI 703

Strolling on Bowling Green Street, once home to Robert Day's factory, where leather goods and saddles were handmade. They were later renowned for their fishing tackle and handmade fishing lures.

Winthrop Street was an extremely busy street at the time when cars and pedestrians shared the roadway. Tylers shoe shops had many branches in the city, including Patrick's Street and North Main Street. A Ford Anglia is driving up the street whilst a Volkswagen Variant is at the front of the row of parked cars.

Above: Passing in front of Cash's, this gentleman was possibly on his way to post his parcel at the GPO on Oliver Plunkett Street.

Right: Outside the iron entrance gates to St Francis's church on North Main Street, a child sits on the bonnet of this badly dented Mark I Cortina as the family wait for someone.

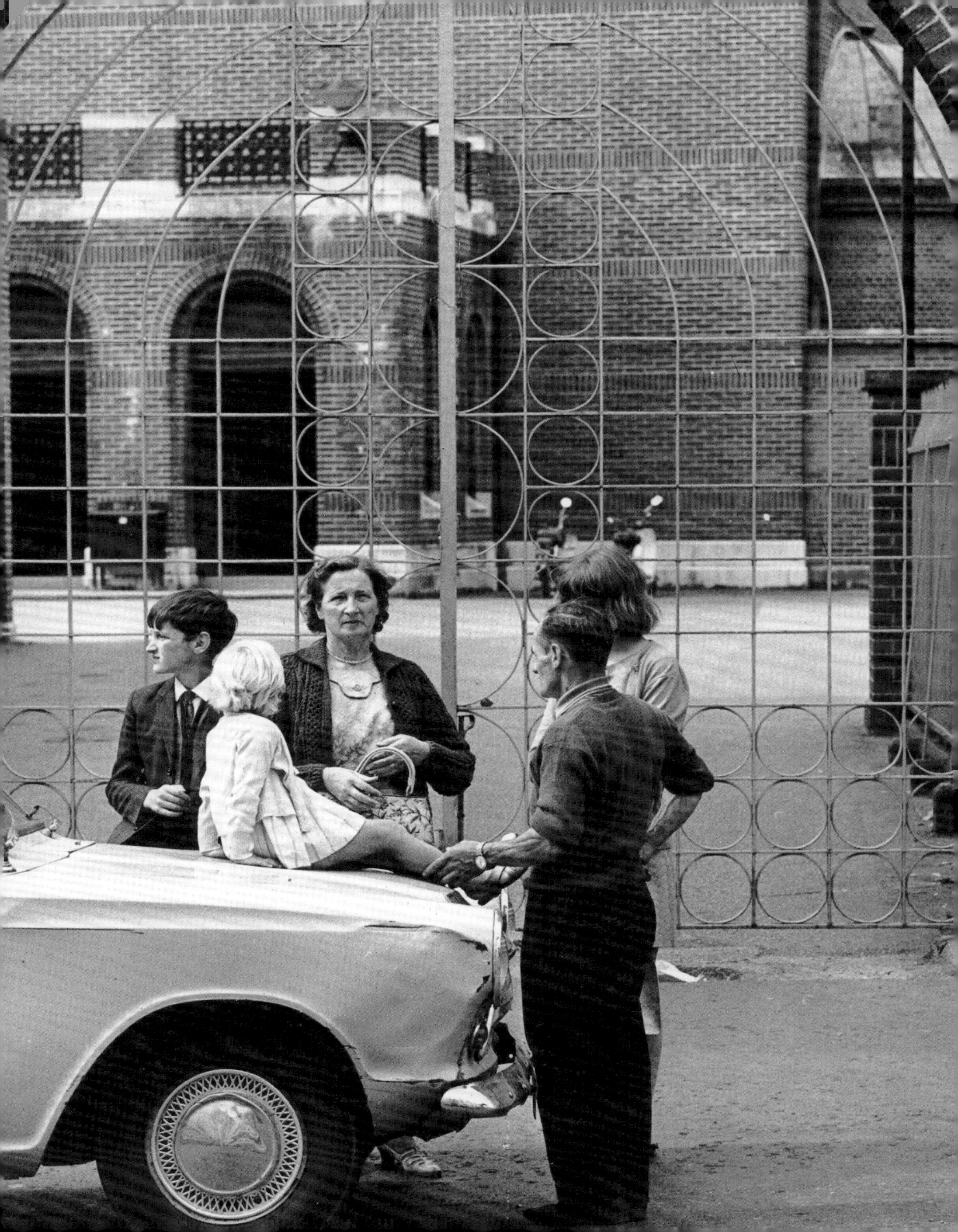

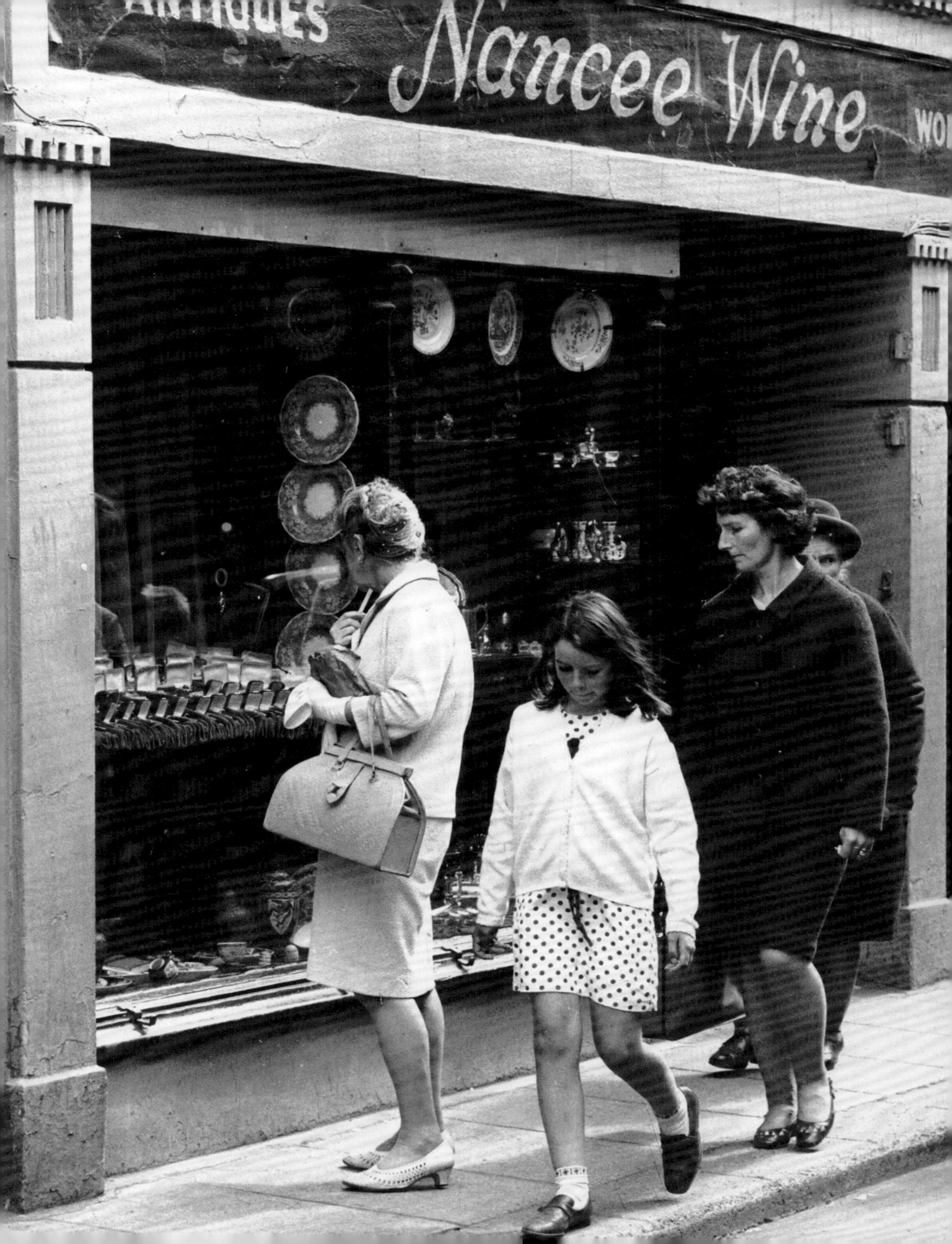
Nancee Wine

Above: Weighing potatoes on an old Avery weighing scales on the Coal Quay, whilst an onlooker watches. The old tea chests have travelled the globe from Ceylon to end their days as table props. May Duggan is the dealer weighing the potatoes outside No. 42, Kearney's restaurant.

Left: A woman is interested in the antique plates, silver and jewellery on display at Nancee Wine's antiques shop, 8 Winthrop Street.

Above: This child is quite happy being wheeled through Dalton's Alley, once home to one of Cork's favourite characters, Kathy Barry. Kathy was renowned for her illicit spirits and crubeens. At the bottom right of the alley is where she had her premises – it was demolished in recent years.

Left: This pipe smoker has stopped for a puff on St Peter and Paul's Place. The steep steps adjoining Thompson's restaurant are long gone.

Above: Finn's Outfitters on Finn's corner, one of Cork's oldest shops, was established in 1858. Canopies like the one on Finn's were a familiar sight over many shopfronts of this era in the city.

Overleaf: An evocative scene of Patrick's Street with the old Christmas lights and traffic at a standstill during the busiest time of the year. The Smith's Stores Anglia van nears its premises and the old *Cork Examiner* display board evokes memories of when the newspaper had its main entrance on Patrick's Street next to Le Château.

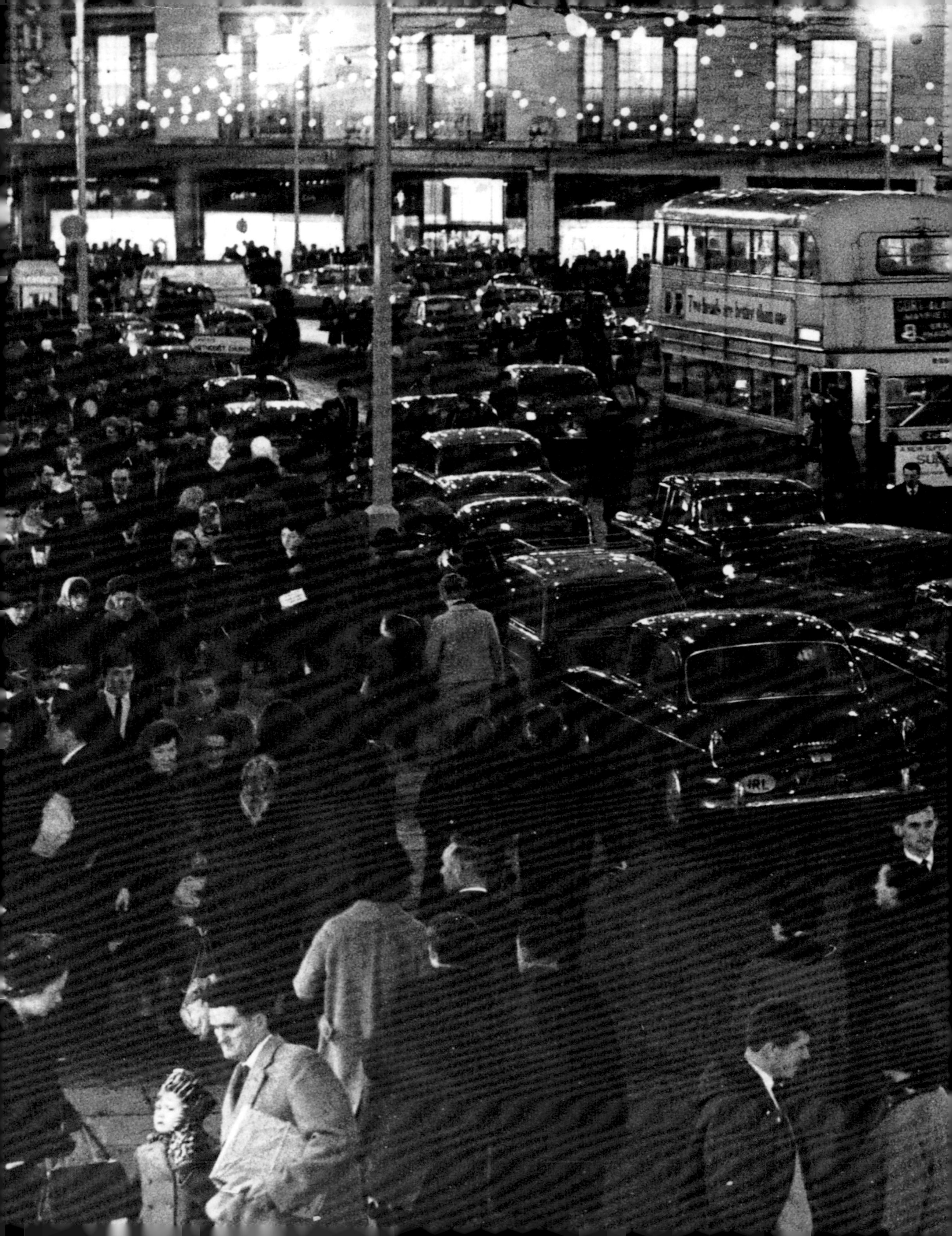

27 28
THE MUNSTER ARC
THE MUNSTER & LEINSTER BANK LTD
SMITHS STORES
Smiths Stores
phone 23051-2-3
OPI 254
ZIF 814
IZB 221
EXAMINER

The bus stop was a convenient place to lean and take the weight off your feet. To the left is John Burke, Solicitor, at 68 South Mall, whilst Jasper Swanton was his neighbouring colleague at a time when this profession was prominent in the South Mall.

A family outing – everybody appears to have time to stop and have a full-scale conversation, even if they are blocking the footpath. In the background are Cudmore's, Burton's and Fitzgerald's tailors.

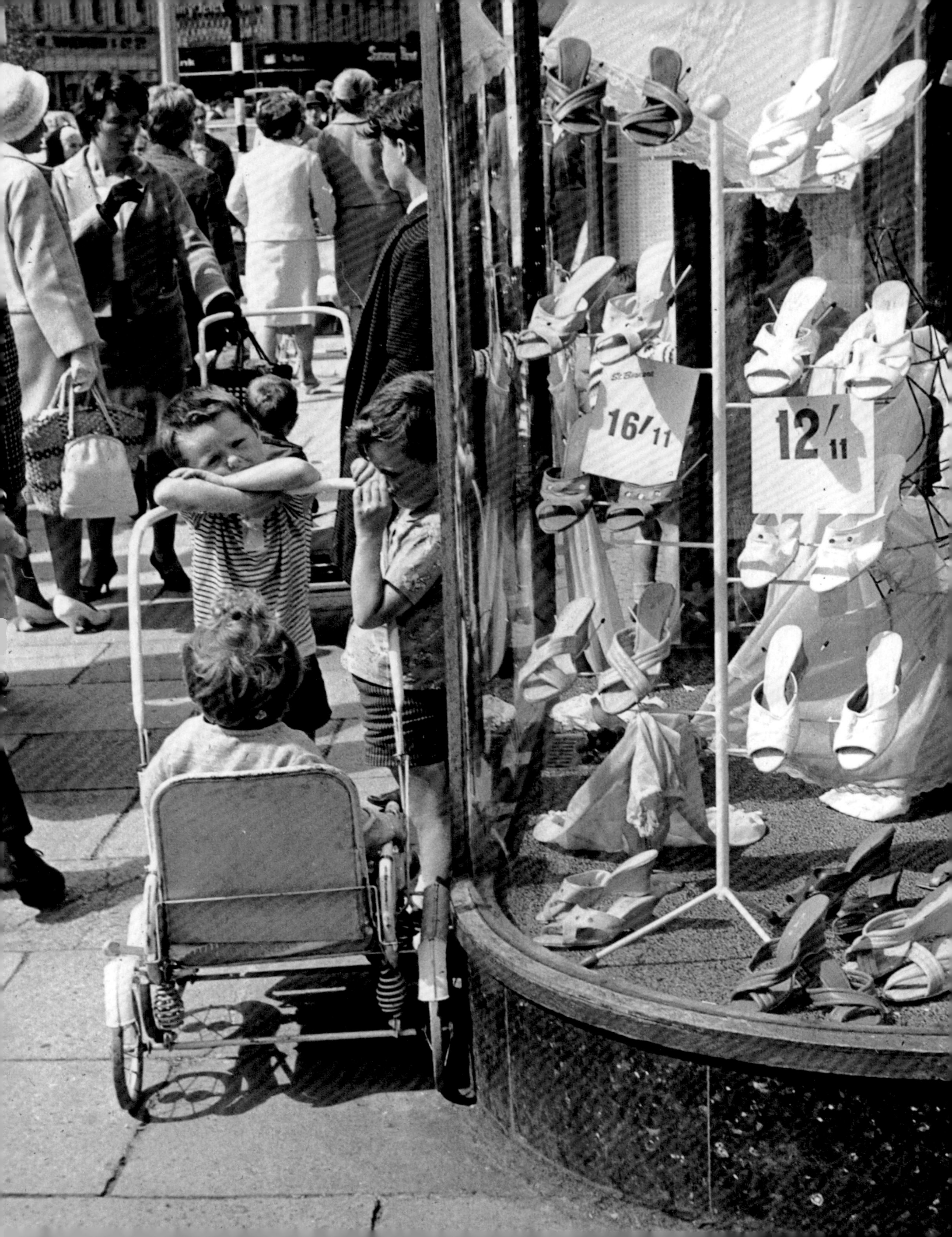
16/11
12/11

Above: A handy resting place outside the old Wesleyan chapel on Patrick's Street.

Left: Bored to tears as mother shops.

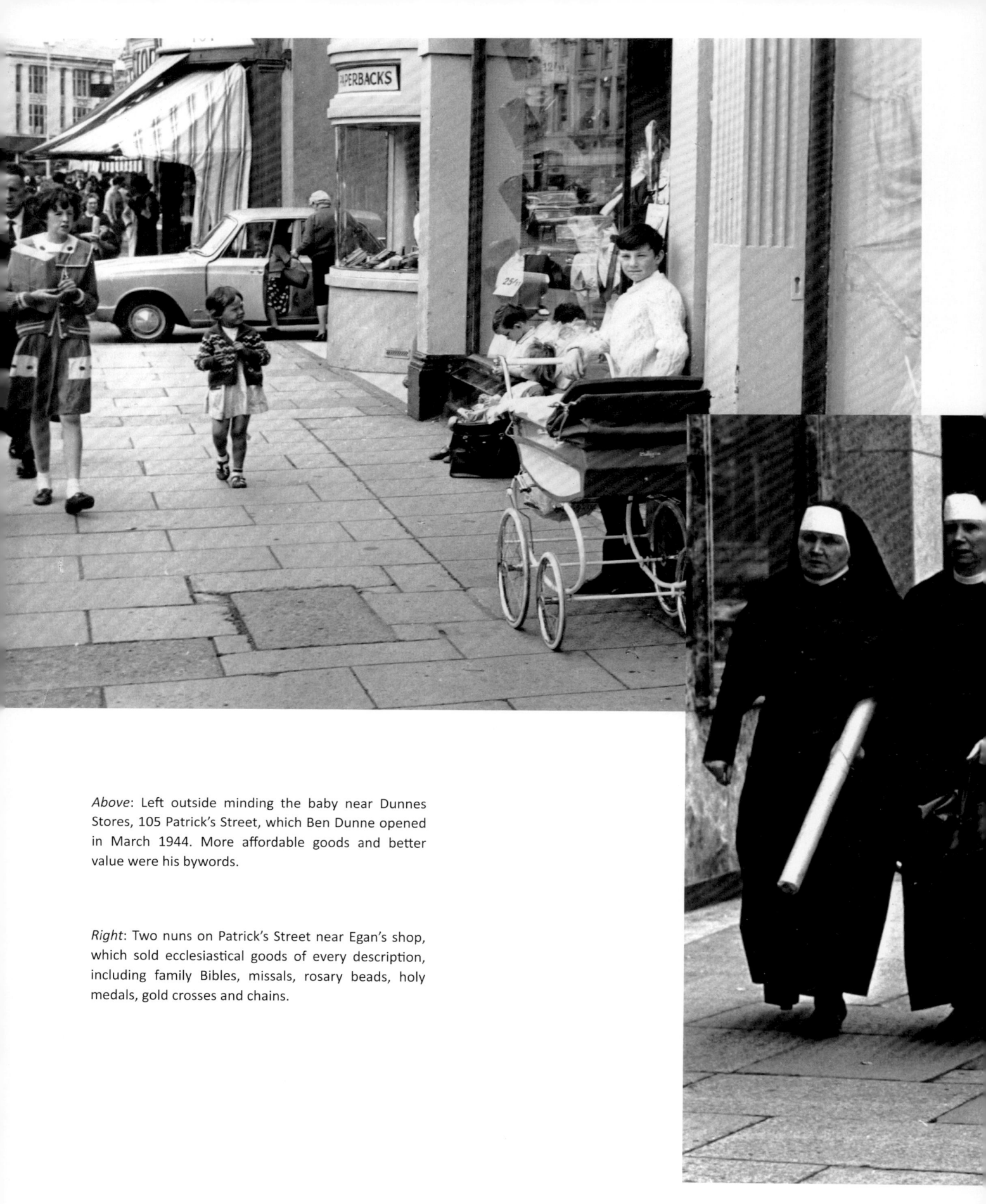

Above: Left outside minding the baby near Dunnes Stores, 105 Patrick's Street, which Ben Dunne opened in March 1944. More affordable goods and better value were his bywords.

Right: Two nuns on Patrick's Street near Egan's shop, which sold ecclesiastical goods of every description, including family Bibles, missals, rosary beads, holy medals, gold crosses and chains.

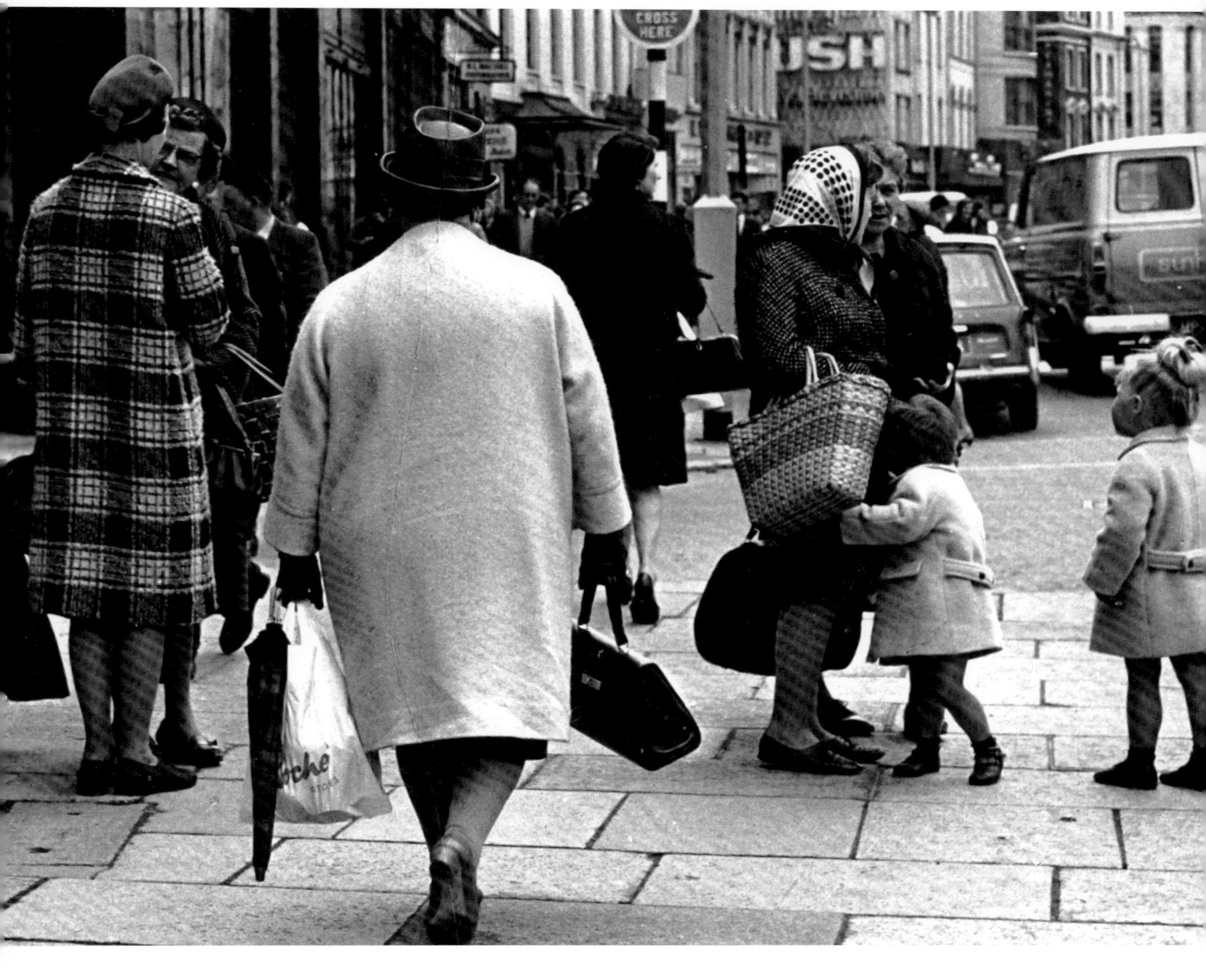
CROSS
HERE

A complete contrast between the young and the old as two young boys stare at the old lady in her shawl. In the background is the temporary Bailey bridge which was put in place during the construction of the new North Gate Bridge (Griffith Bridge) to allow access from Bachelor's Quay to the North Mall. It was Anthony Barry, who held the position of Lord Mayor at the time, who opened the new bridge on 6 November 1961.

This posed picture shows brothers Andrew (*left*) and James Doherty (*right*) proudly showing off their Airedale dogs.

A fine selection of electrical goods at Electrical & Radio Services, 40 Prince's Street, the main agents for Philips, now trading as Murphy Electrical. A girl with a pram waits patiently outside.

Two women wait in the doorway of Fred Archer, silversmith and jeweller, at 67 Patrick's Street, also home to Stephen J. Scully, a Chartered Quantity Surveyor.

Above: A complete contrast: two women wearing trouser suits – the very height of 1960s fashion – pass another woman wearing a polka-dot headscarf on Patrick's Street.

Right: Two elderly ladies enjoying a good gossip.

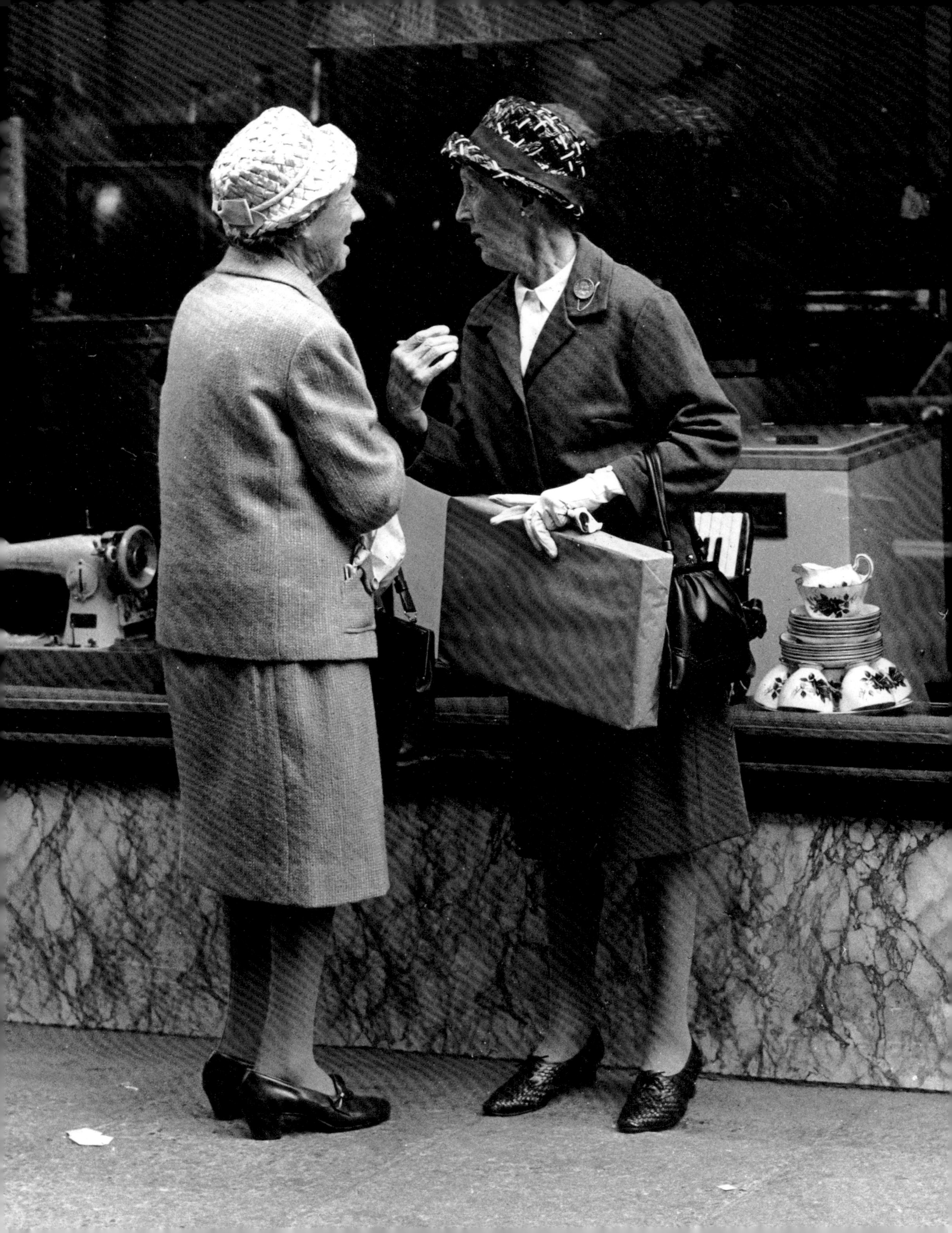

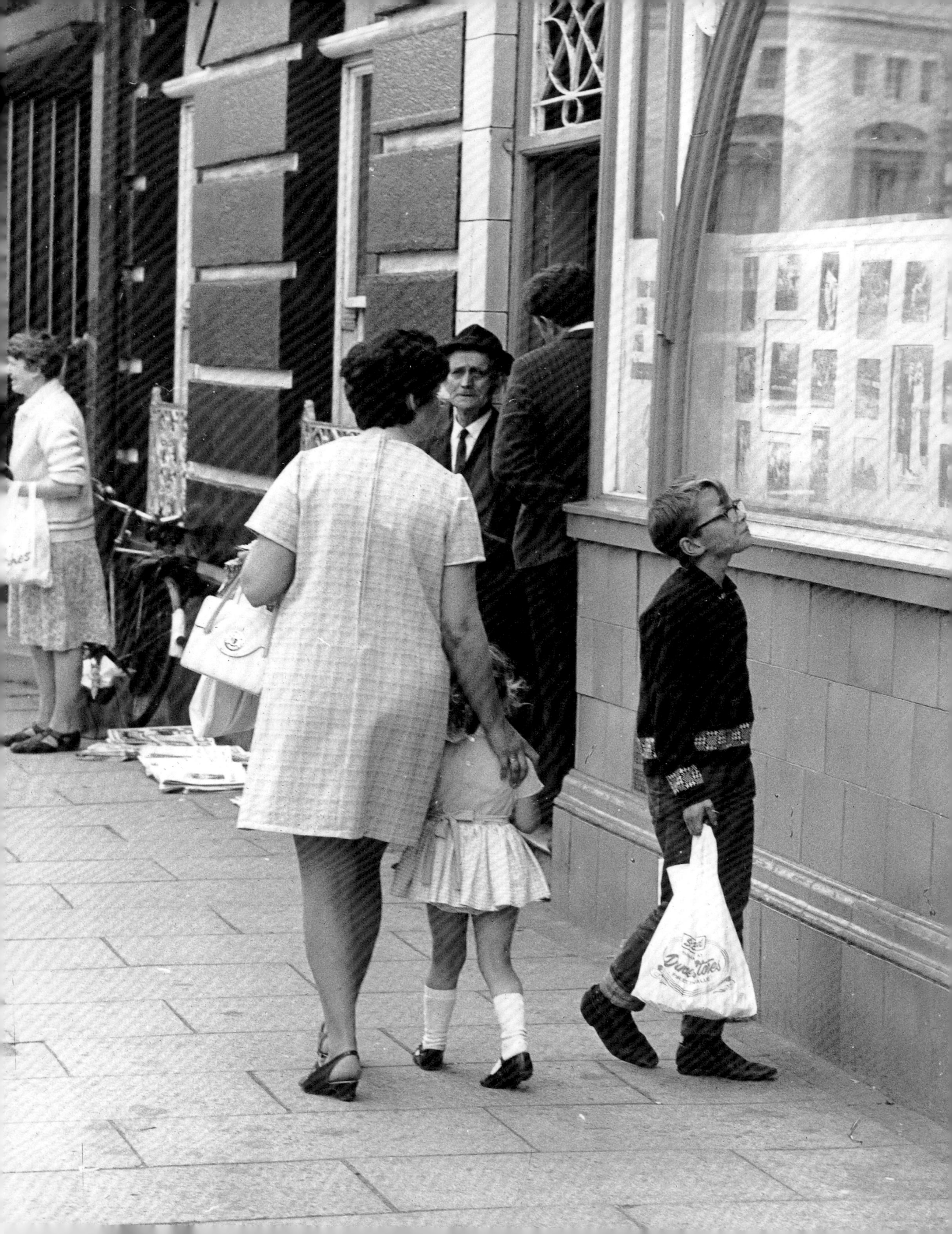

Above: Three girls reading the *Cork Examiner*. In the background a cyclist looks on as an NSU car passes him. NSU was a German car and motorcycle manufacturer that was later taken over by Audi.

Left: A boy looking at the *Independent* press photographs displayed in the window of their offices at 37 Patrick's Street. In the background a newspaper seller has his papers on the ground near the Victoria Hotel.

Above: Having a lark outside Cash's, which is displaying goods on the last day of the sales. On the left is Pa Mulcahy and carrying the parcel is Billy Venner. Cash's was a very popular shop which hosted many sales during the year, including their remnant, bonanza and white sales of top quality merchandise at great discounts.

Right: This girl does not seem amused to have been left minding her mother's shopping outside Guinness House on Patrick's Street.

Overleaf: The Coal Quay, where anything from a needle to an anchor could be bought. Bedsteads, chairs and vegetables are on display. The woman wearing the white headscarf to the right of the chair is Mrs Twomey. The Coal Quay dealer under the centre arch of Clayton Love's, gesticulating with her hands, is Mary O'Leary.

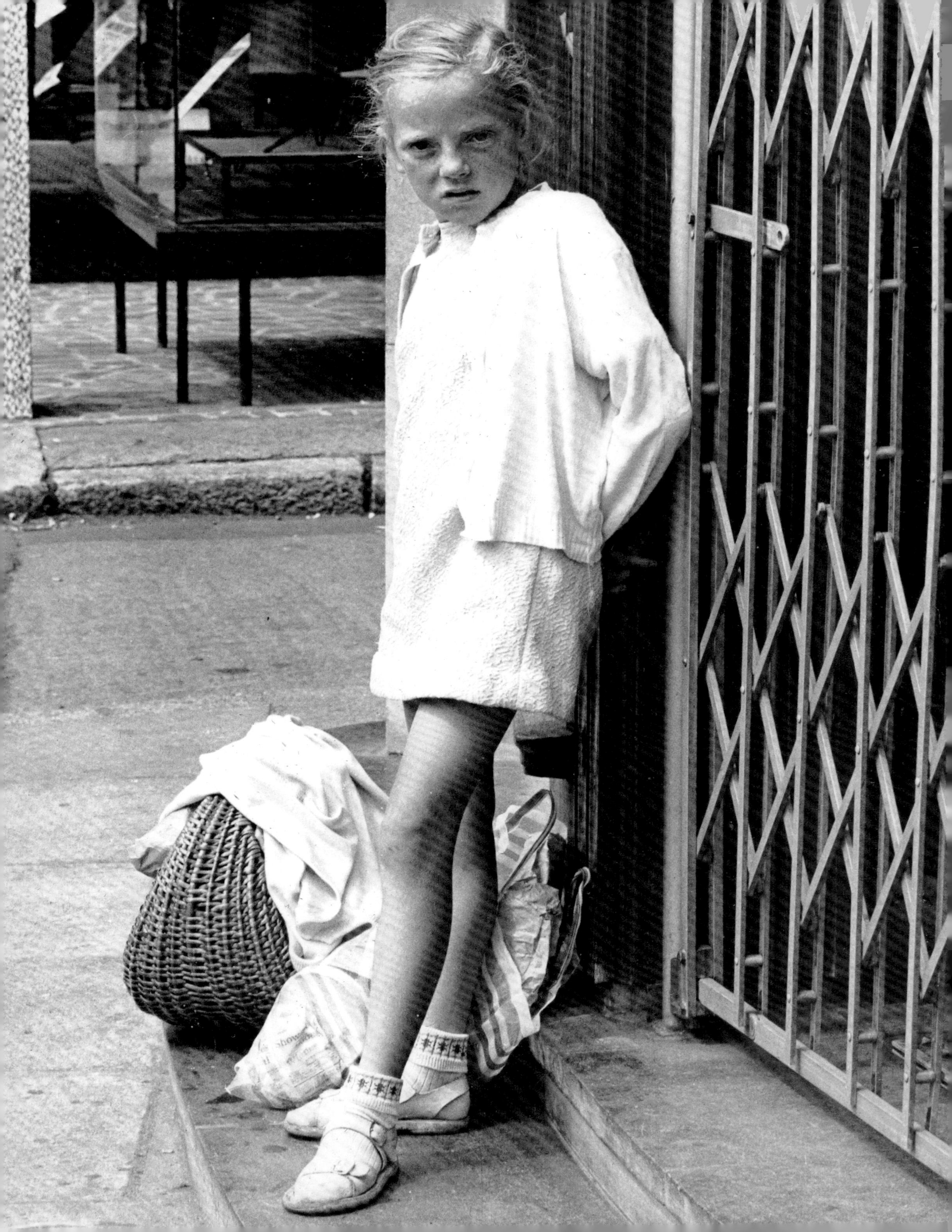

LAYTON LOVE

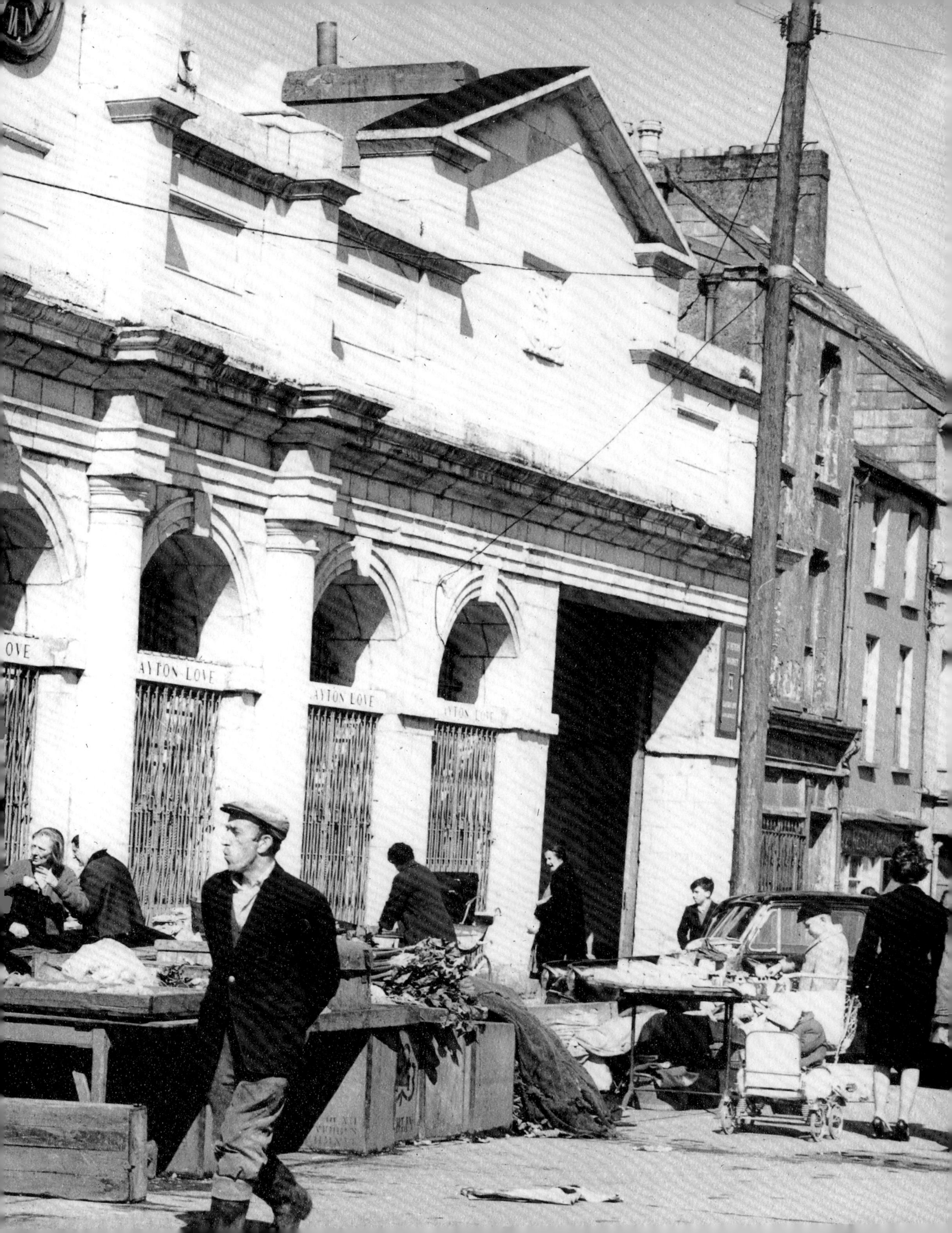
OVE
AYTON LOVE
AYTON LOVE
AYTON LOVE

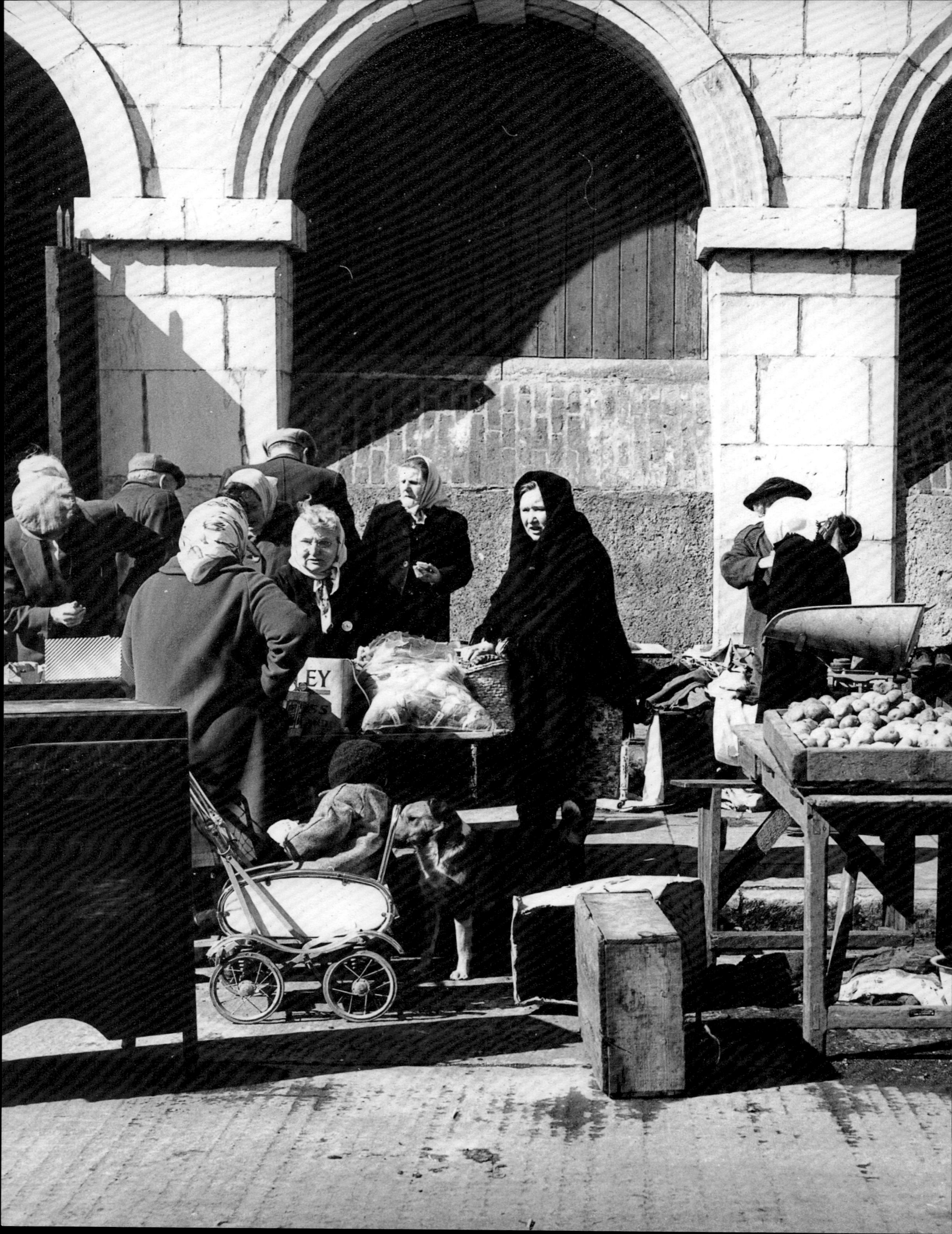
EY

Above: I want that one! A wonderful display of model cars and lorries in John Roche's, Patrick's Street. The toy shop window is strategically placed at a perfect height for small children.

Left: The traditional shawl so long associated with the street traders on the Coal Quay was often purchased from the Queens Old Castle on the nearby Grand Parade. Mrs Twomey is facing the camera wearing a white headscarf. To her right, in the shawl is Francis Twomey. In the background wearing a headscarf is Laurie Connors.

Above: Two people looking in the window of the *Examiner* office, Academy Street. Le Château, behind, had three entrances – on Academy Street, Patrick's Street and Faulkner's Lane.

Right: A gentleman relaxes near a sign for the ladies toilet close to Cork Opera House. The toilet was the brainchild of a Cork city councillor and well-known character by the name of Klondyke, who canvassed successfully for its construction.

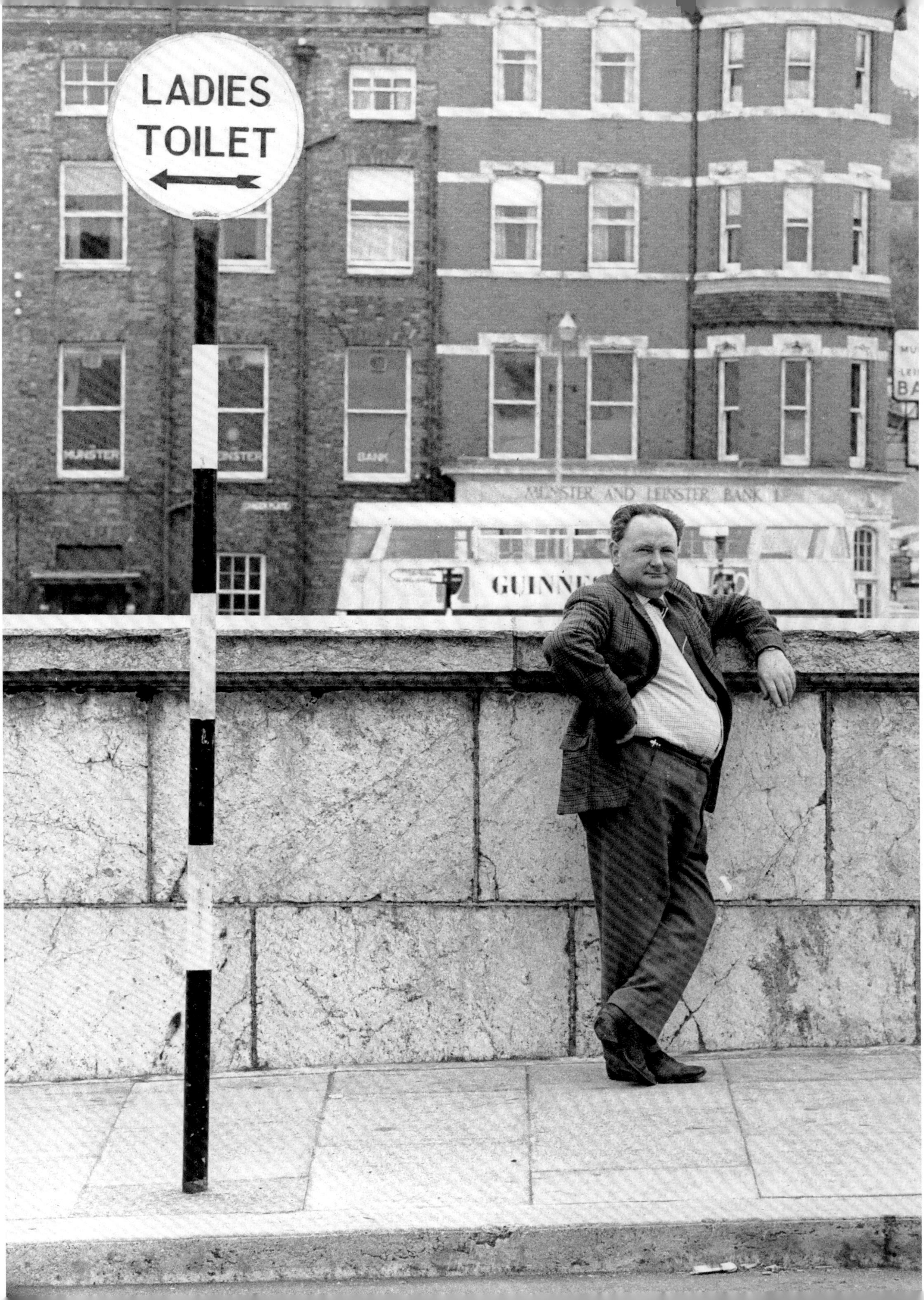
LADIES
TOILET
MUNSTER AND LEINSTER BANK

Above: Waiting for a bus on Patrick's Street. The shop in the background was once owned by Liptons and later became part of the Five Star supermarket chain.

Right: At the top of Patrick's Street this fashionable lady is totally engrossed in the paper – life was less frenetic in the 1960s.

Overleaf: These two pictures show the contrasting sides of life in 1960s Cork. In one two nuns in their traditional garb stop for a chat with a friend outside Egan's ecclesiastical department, while in the other we see two ladies dressed in the very height of fashion – one with a plaid skirt complete with matching wide tie, the other in designer tights, although she still sports the more traditional headscarf.

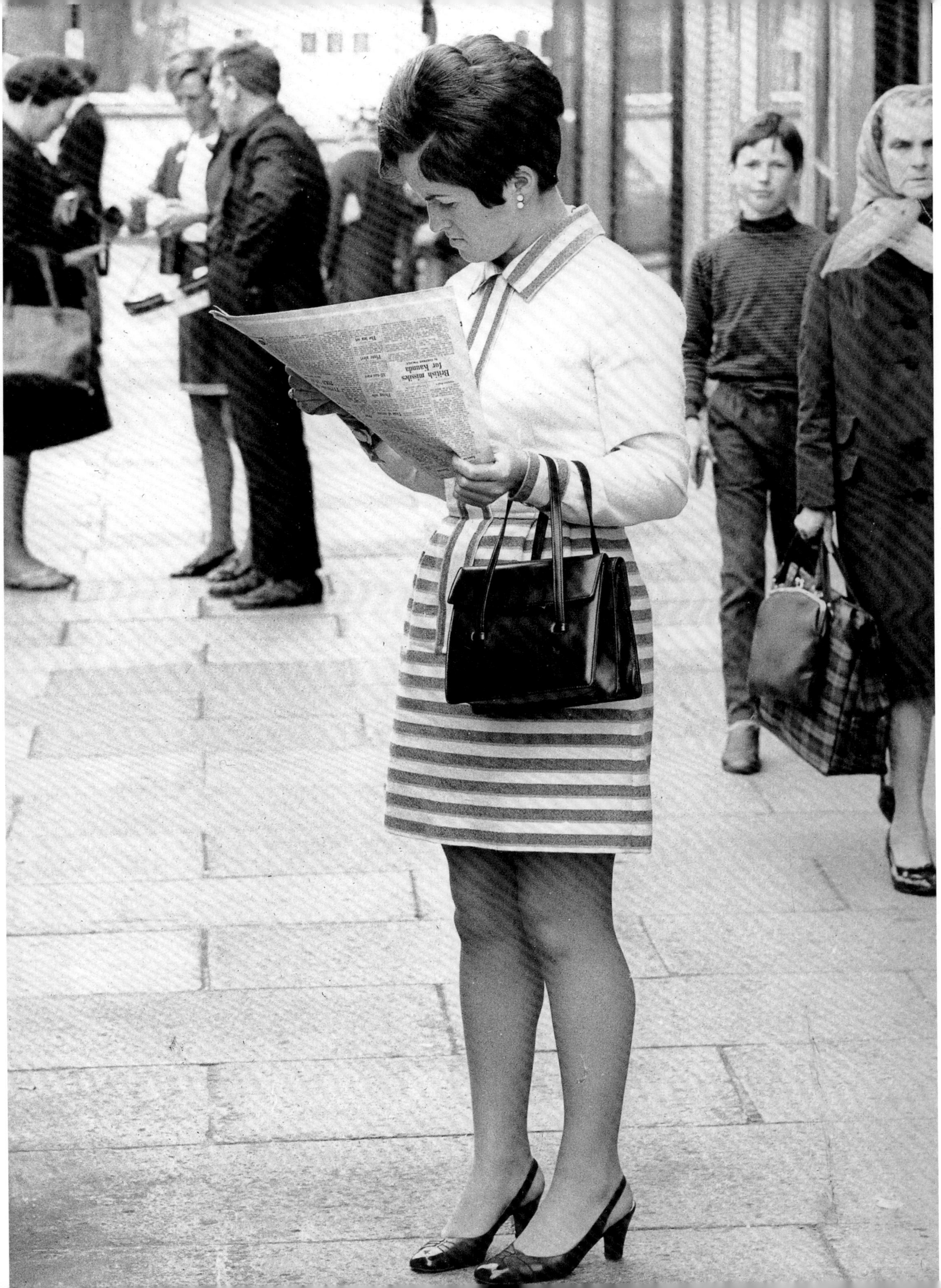
British missiles
for Kaunda

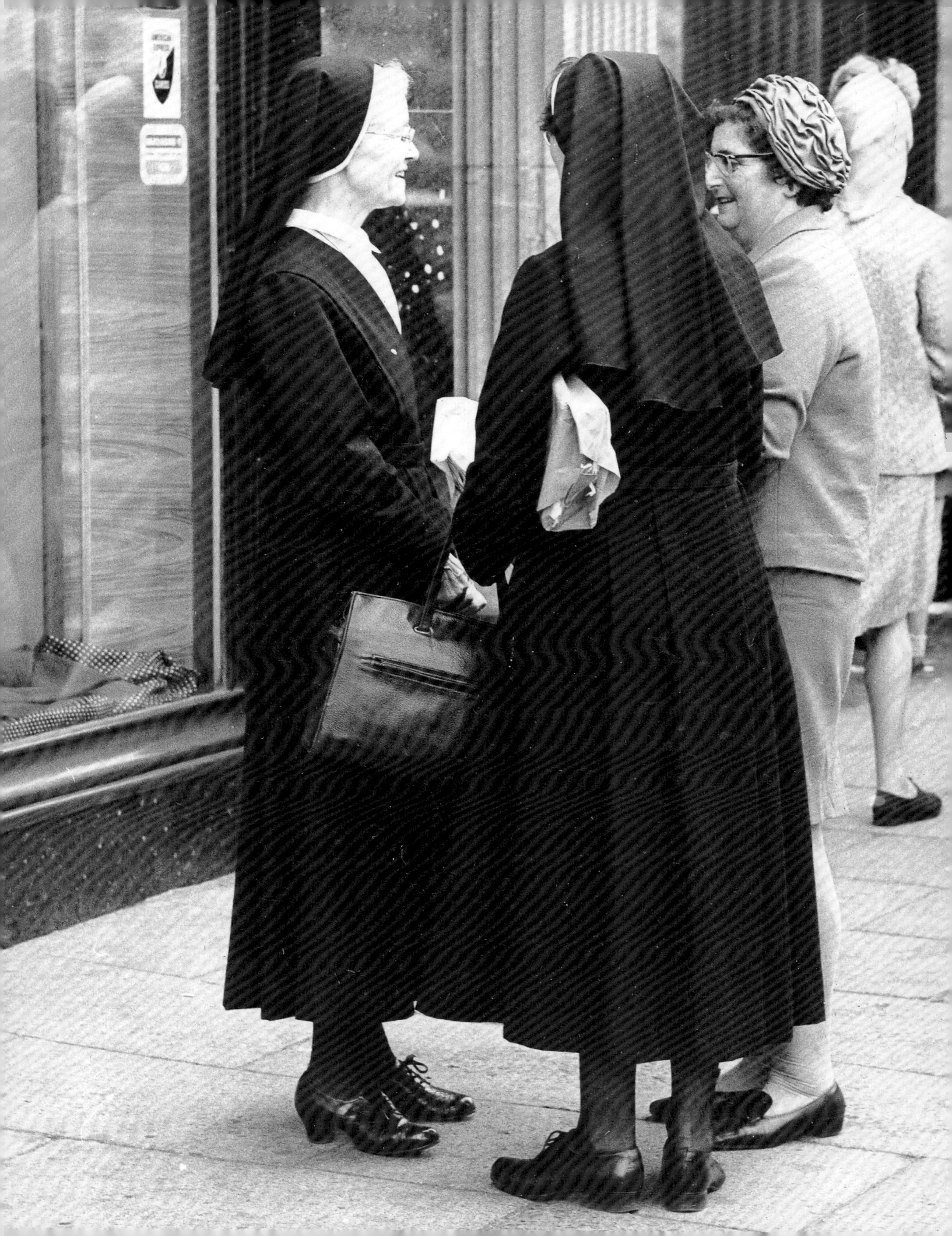

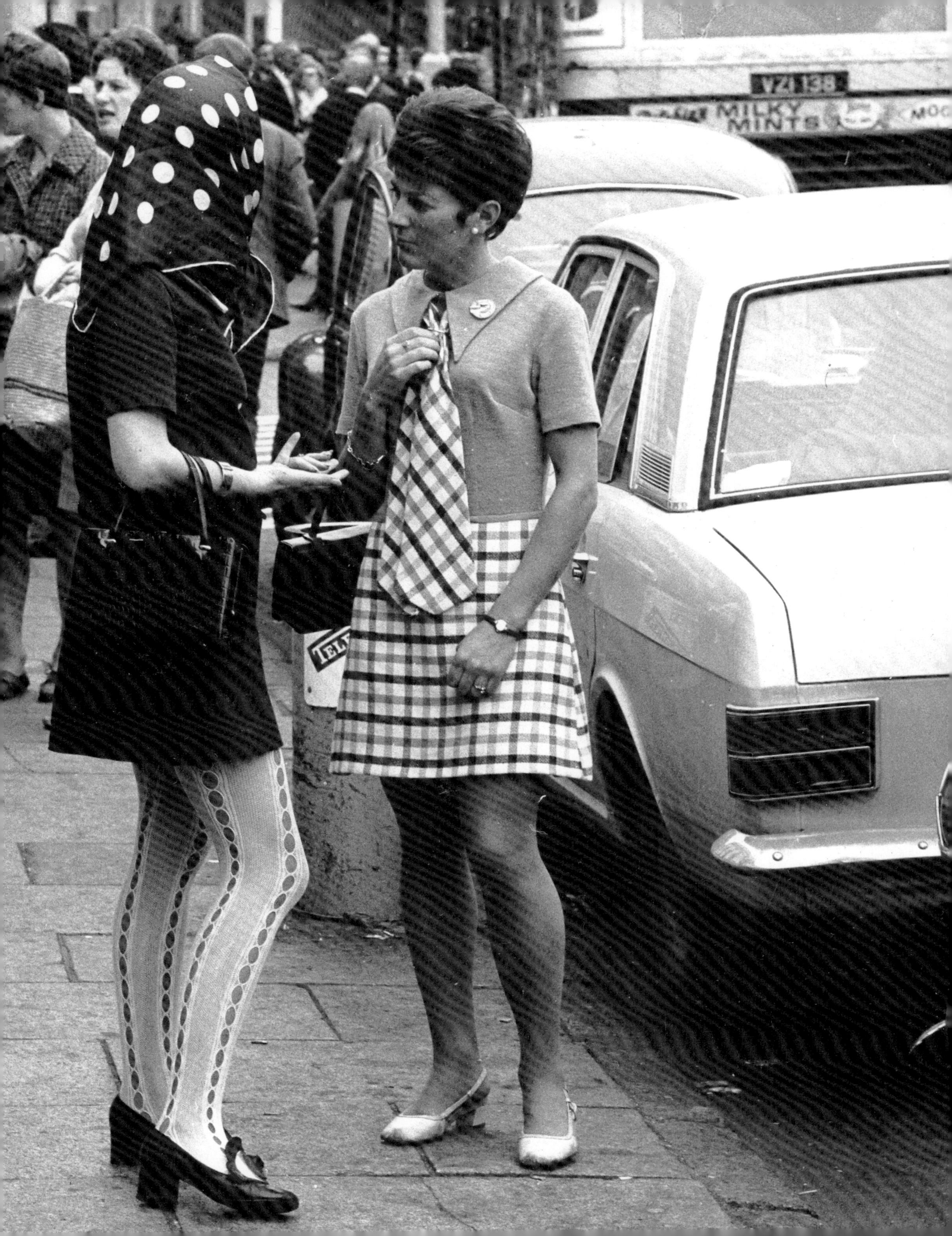
VZI 138
MILKY MINTS

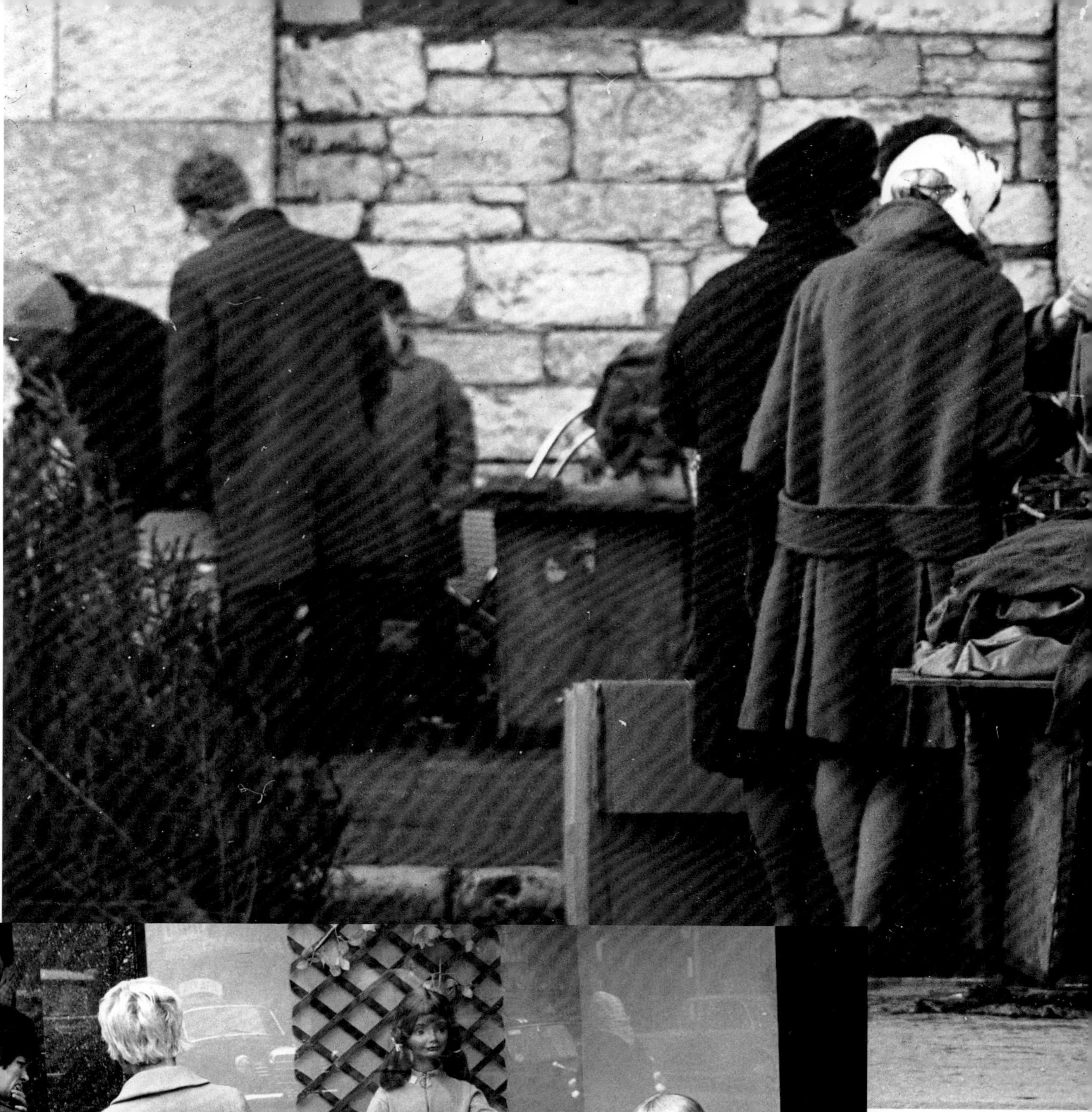
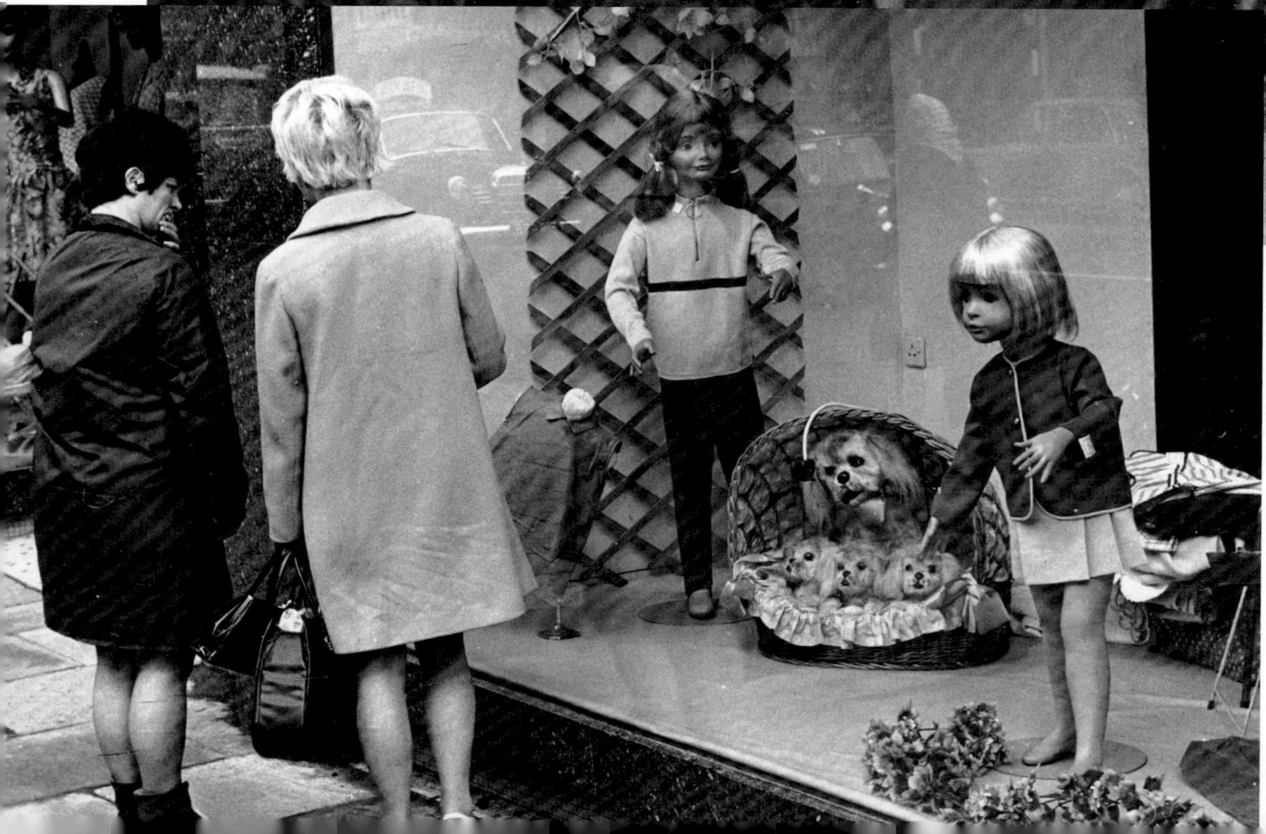

Above: A lively trading scene on the Coal Quay. The pram to the right is laden with more clothes, so there is certainly no shortage of stock. The woman in the centre, selling her wares, is Iris Casey.

Left: How much is that doggie in the window?

Cycling was a popular mode of transport judging by the bicycles outside St Augustine's church on Washington Street after Mass.

Barry's shop front on Prince's Street. Barry's has been a part of Cork tradition since 1901, as every discerning Cork tea drinker knows. Winning the prestigious Empire Cup for tea blending in 1934 was a great achievement. Their motto at the time was 'Barry's Tea: as well known as Shandon!'

This gentleman stands outside a restaurant on Patrick's Street waiting for a friend, complete with traditional flat cap and suit. The reflection on the doorway reveals that it is located near Roches Stores.

Queuing for a bus outside the limestone façade of the National Bank, South Mall, which also had a branch on Patrick's Street.

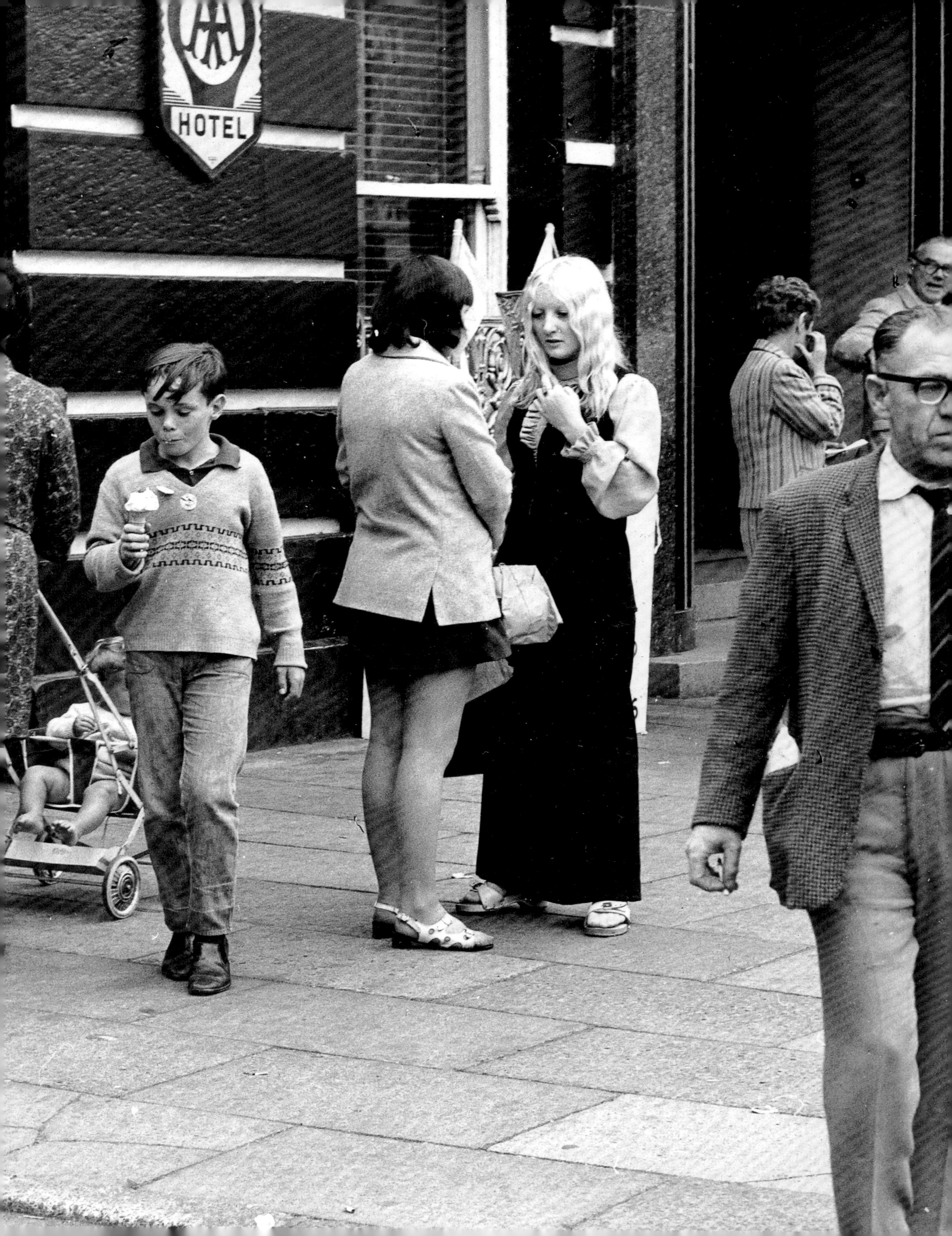
HOTEL

Above: Women waiting for a bus laden down with parcels at a bus stop on the South Mall. No. 69 South Mall was home to the well-known Cork architect William Hill.

Left: Enjoying an ice cream outside a very busy Victoria Hotel, which was the oldest hotel in the city until it closed recently; it was constructed in 1810.

Above: This Wallace Express horse and dray driver, outside Tylers shoe shop, seems a little put out by a hold-up in traffic. Horse-drawn transport was coming to an end when this picture was taken, as mechanised transport became the order of the day. The Wallace Express delivery company's stables were located on Union Quay.

Right: Kyle Street was a popular area for trading, with stacks of clothes often strewn on the pavement for onlookers to examine before the haggling began.

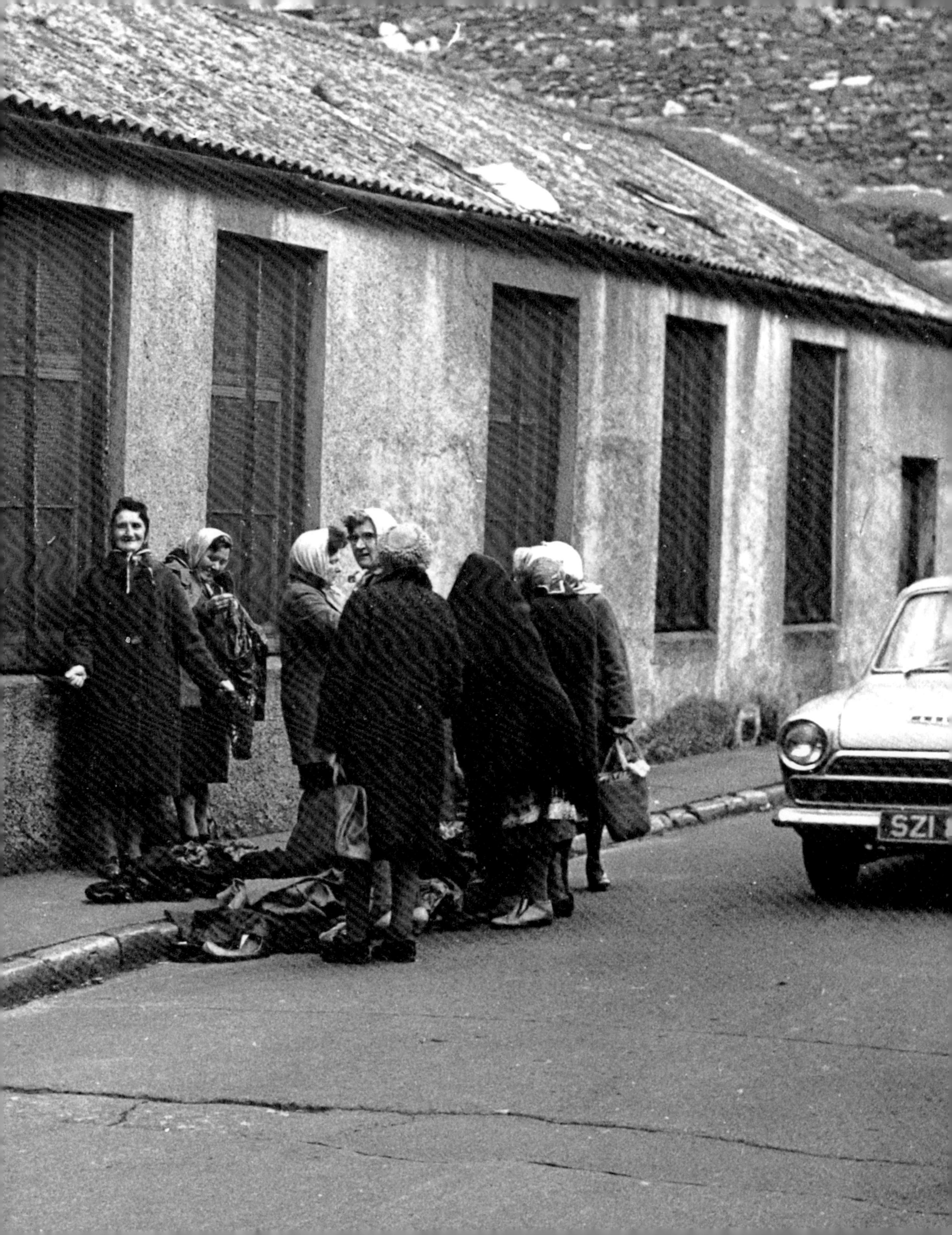
SZI

Above: Cheerful flag sellers, collecting for the West Indian mission, at the corner of the South Mall and Parliament Street. Dan Turner's behind them was a very popular pub in the city.

Right: A boy wearing the mandatory short pants sits on the window sill of a disused shop, while a well-dressed gentleman smokes his pipe and reads the paper.

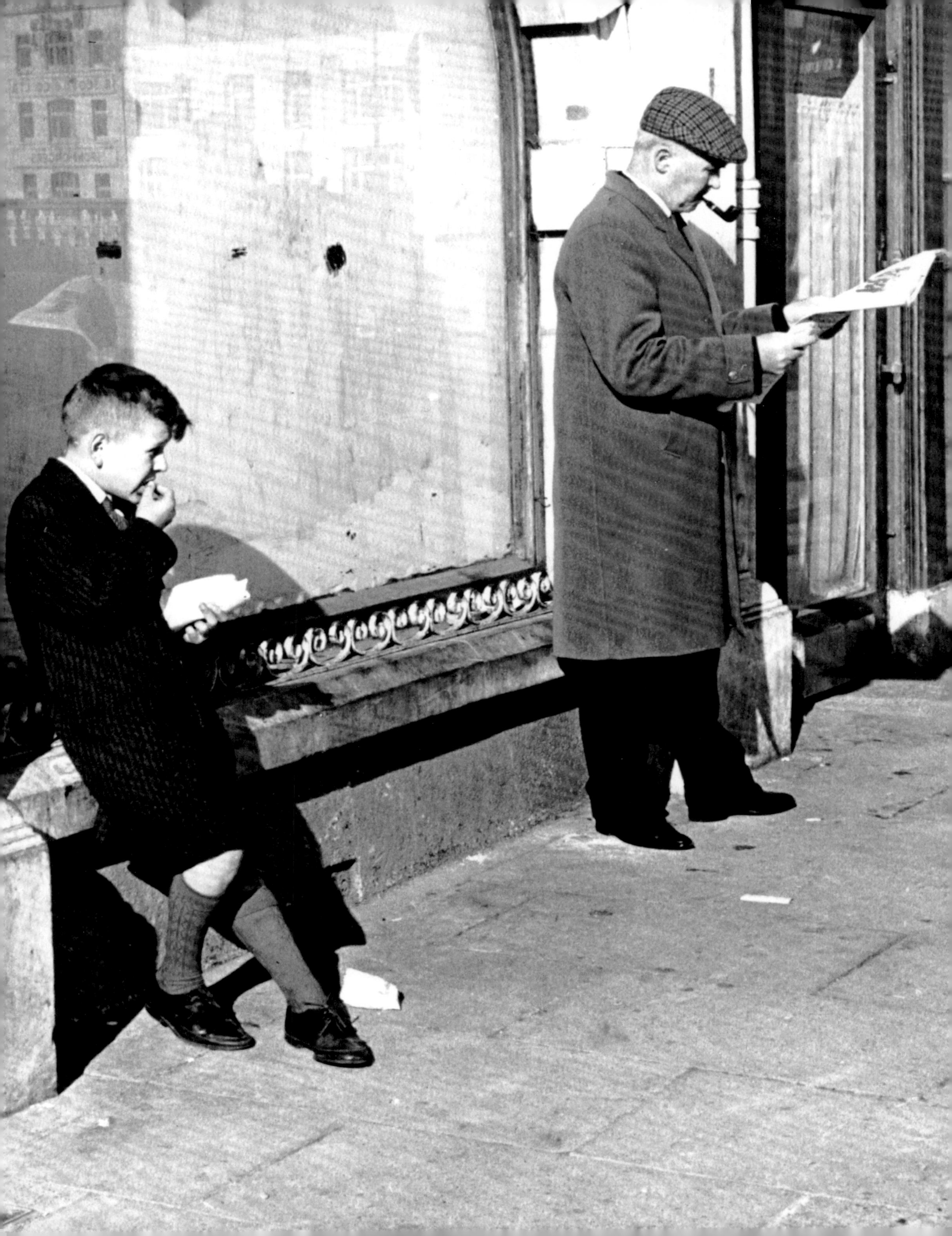

Two women, who appear to be wearing the West Cork cloak, make an ethereal silhouette while walking down Patrick's Street. Parked near the old post box is a Ford Anglia car.

A garda checks the motorbike licence of this Suzuki driver. The main agents for Suzuki (known as the flyweight champion of the world) were Hanover Cycles at 43–44 Oliver Plunkett Street.

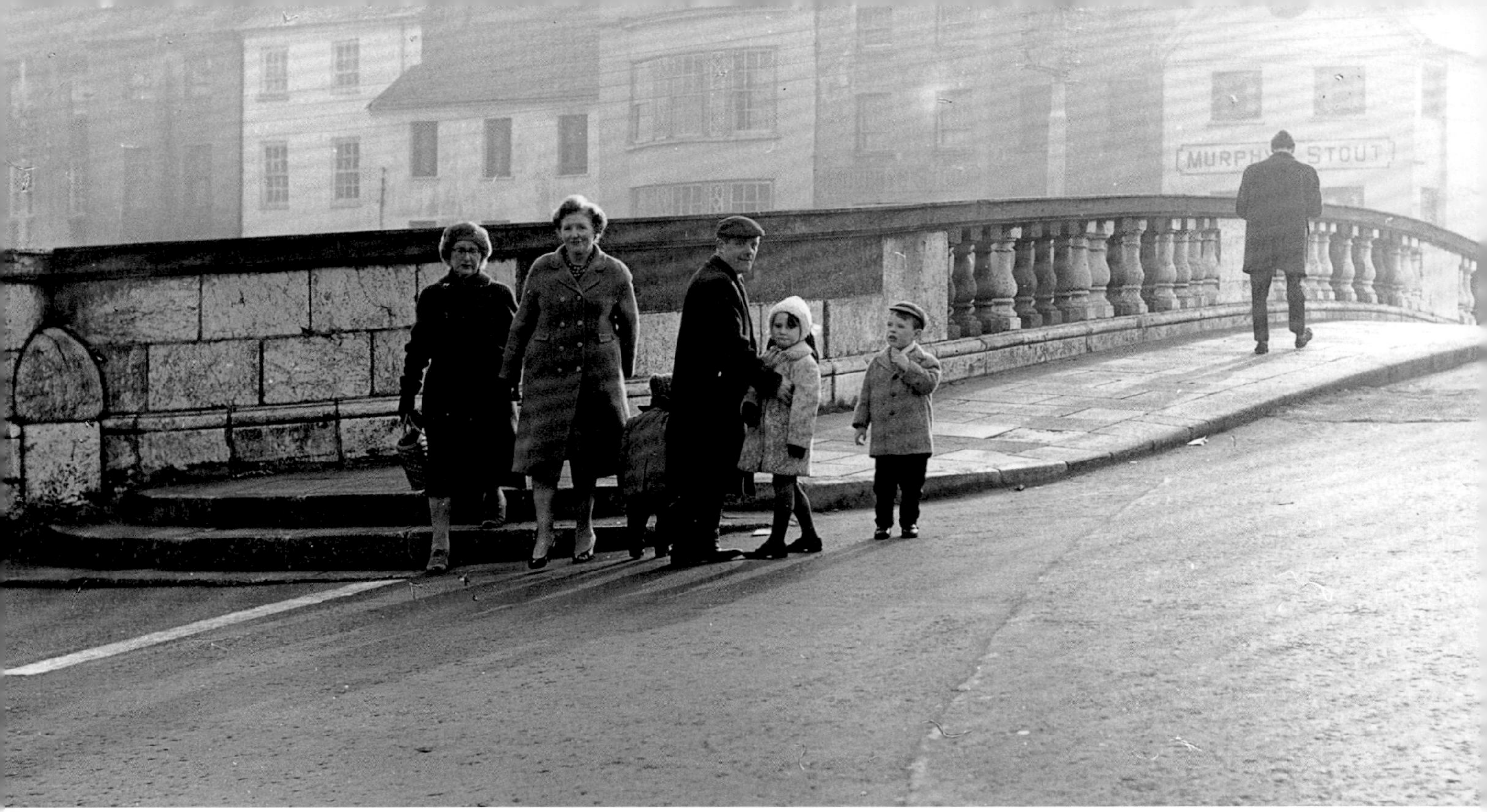
MURPH
STOUT

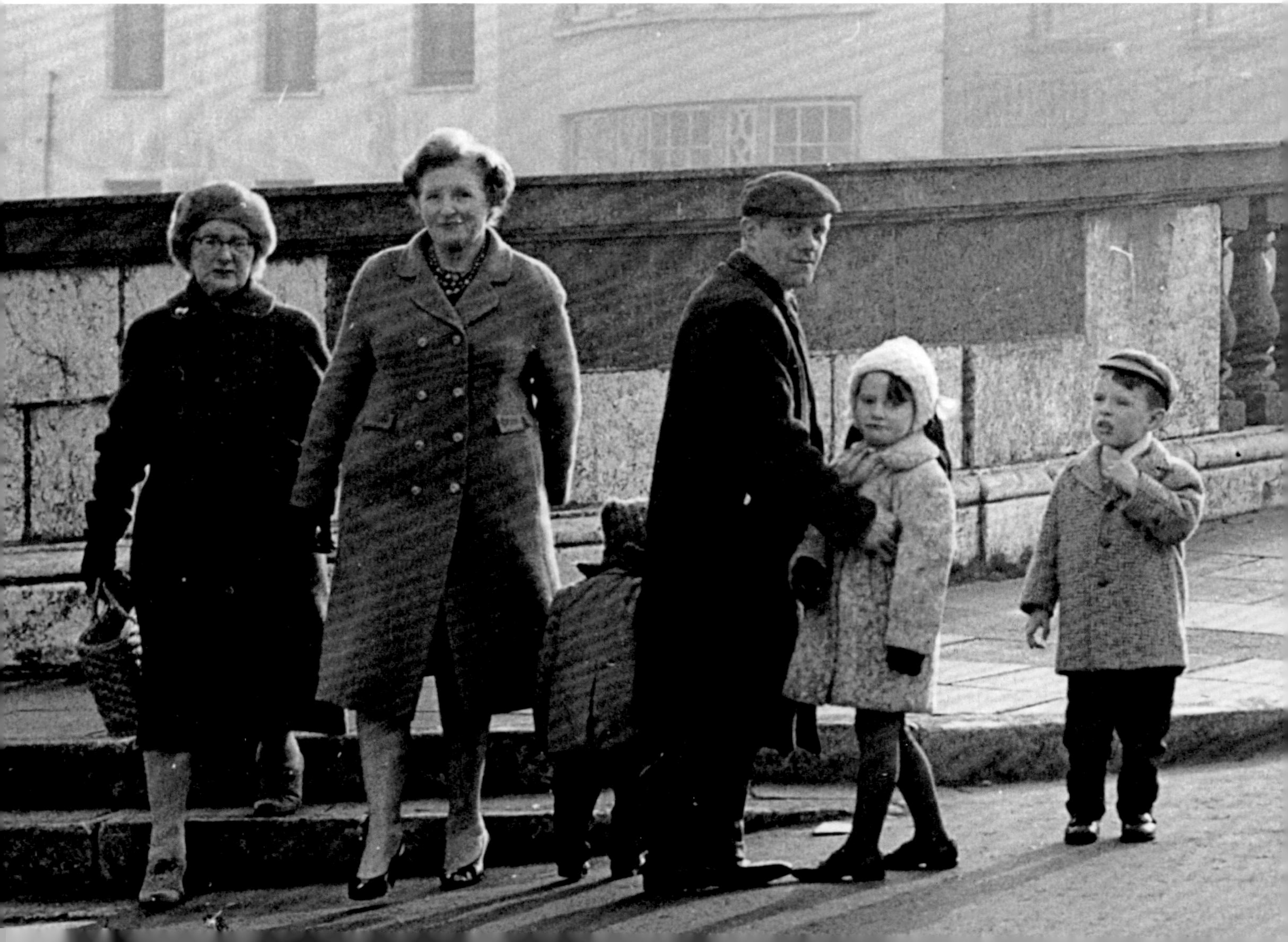

Above: Handing over the bag of customary Thompsons cakes outside this 1-hour dry cleaners. Thompsons had been the most popular cake manufacturers in the city since 1894 – snowballs, chocolate tarts, long doughnuts, custard slices and apple turnovers were just some of the selection available. On the left is Patricia O'Brien, with her sister Chrissie on the right.

Left: A family crossing Parliament Bridge – the old Georgian buildings are a wonderful backdrop. The ornate bridge was built in 1806 at a cost of £4,000.

A man leans on a Morris Minor van. The slogan on Aiden F. Dunne's truck behind states, 'We don't keep the best, we sell it!' The two children in the double go-car are quite unconcerned as they are pushed by Mary Twomey of the nearby Corporation Buildings.

This Cortina estate attracts the attention of some boys, while other pedestrians are more interested in the bargains or betting under the large parasol on the Coal Quay. This area was also host to an escape artist and a performer who lay on a bed of nails.

Above: The main bus station in Parnell Place, where passengers make their way towards their transport. Both buses carry ads for competing Irish stout brands: apparently 'It's a long day that has no Guinness' but 'Beamish is better!'

Right: A little girl does her share of minding her brother.

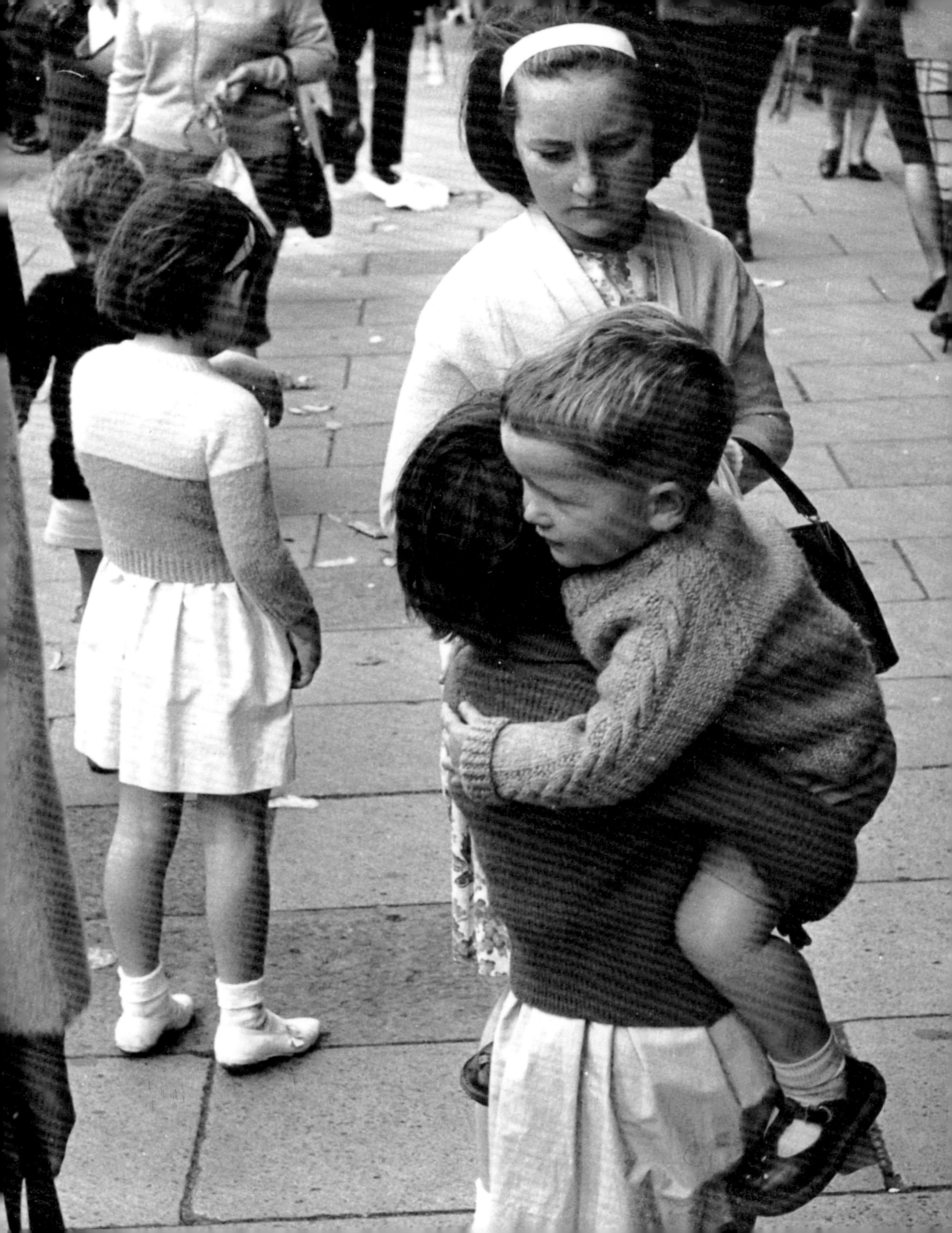

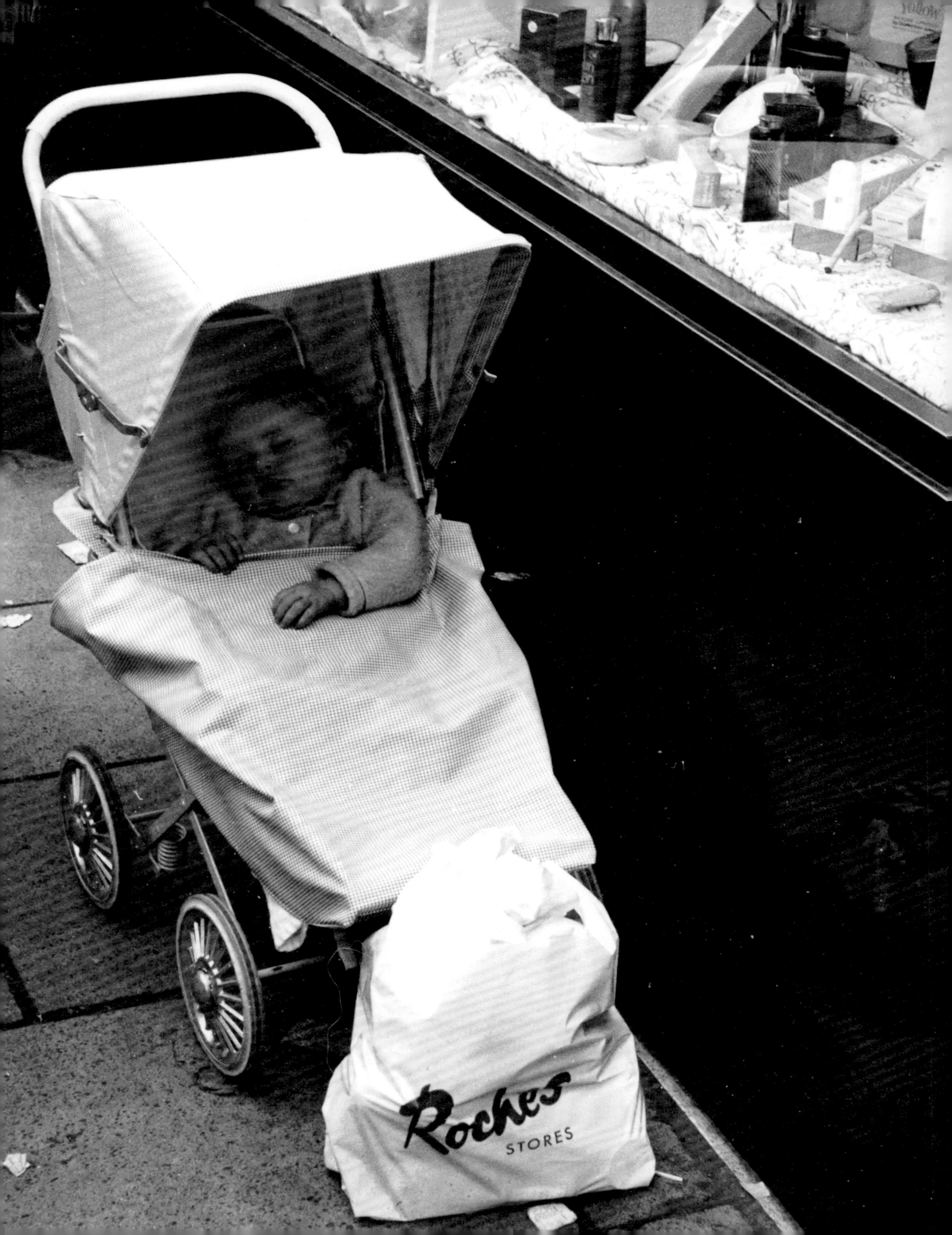
Roches
STORES

Above: Schoolgirls wearing their uniform which was composed of the traditional pinafore and stockings.

Left: A child sleeps soundly in its buggy outside Lester's chemist shop, 106–107 Patrick's Street. These were clearly more trusting times as a heavily laden Roches Stores bag has also been temporarily abandoned.

Above: The old Cork airport where you could watch the planes take off and land from the open balcony. The first flight from the airport was from Cork to Dublin, return, on 16 October 1961, on a plane chartered by the firm of Jacob's biscuits. The lady facing the camera wearing a coat is Rita Barry, wife of Anthony Barry.

Right: The Savoy cinema on Patrick's Street, where two men on top of a very tall stepladder change light bulbs. The Savoy opened on 12 May 1932 and it was Cork's largest, most stylish cinema, holding an audience in excess of 2,000 people. Cork's first international film festival was held here in 1956 and quickly became one of the most prestigious festivals in the world.

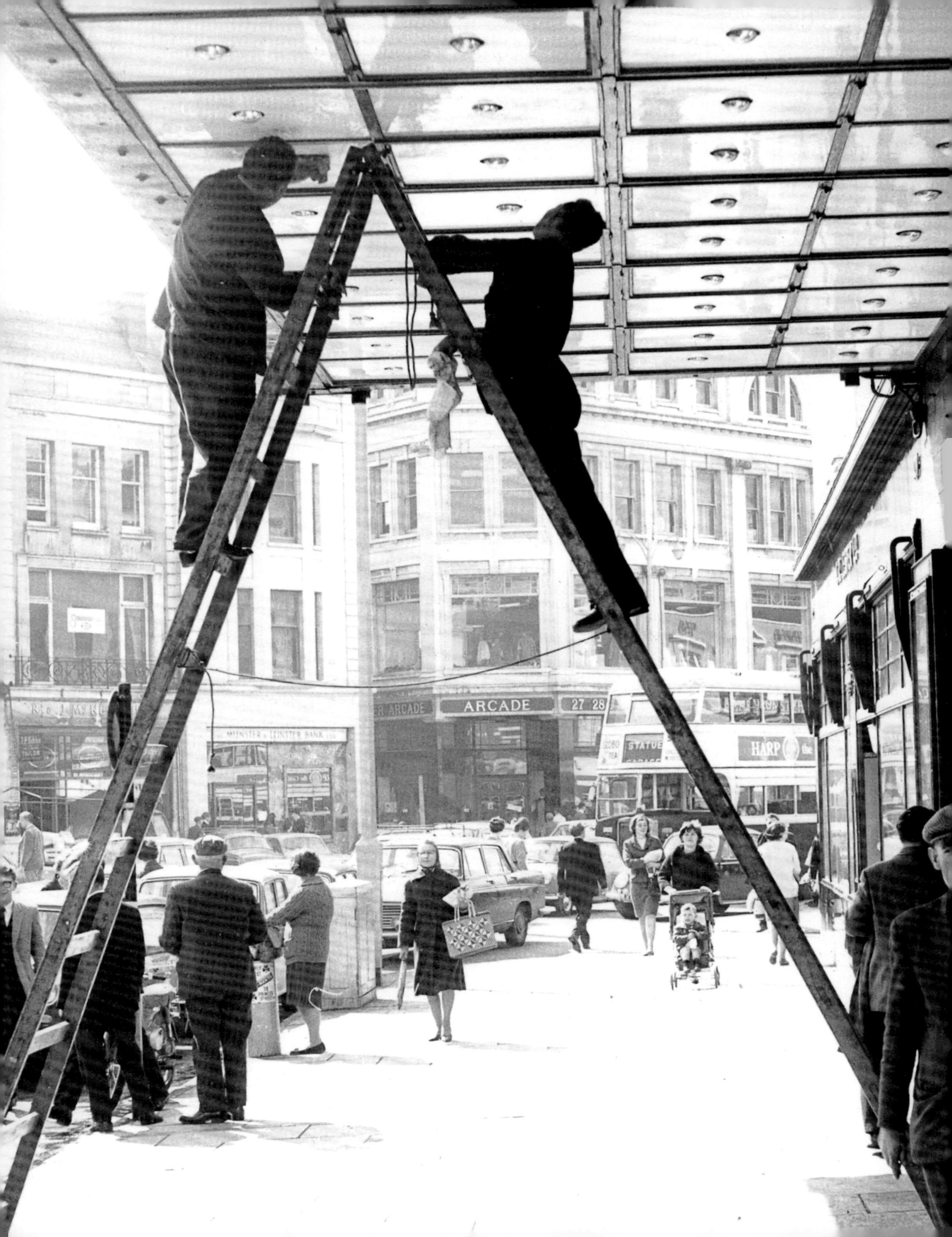
ARCADE
27 28
MUNSTER & LEINSTER BANK
STATUE
HARP

Messenger boys bikes were a common sight in Cork; many a young lad delivered messages to the more opulent addresses in Douglas, Blackrock and Montenotte. Some of these daredevils raced down Patrick's Hill at breakneck speed with little regard for life or limb. In the background are the Cactus Chinese Restaurant, Burton's, Fitzgerald's and McKechnie's cleaners and dyers.

The Arcadia dance hall, fondly known to generations of Corkonians as the Arc, featured some of the finest bands in Ireland and the UK down through the decades. These posters advertise The Drifters, The Kingpins and The Californians show bands. It is hard to imagine that superstars such as Rory Gallagher and U2 also played there.

Above: A street scene at the top corner of the Grand Parade. The large square canopy near the telephone box was where the old Capital cinema existed. The distinctive building on the corner was O'Callaghan's chemists.

Right: This child rides her tricycle outside 3 Cornmarket Street, which was home to Mintern antiques. For many years Cork had a wonderful selection of antique shops.

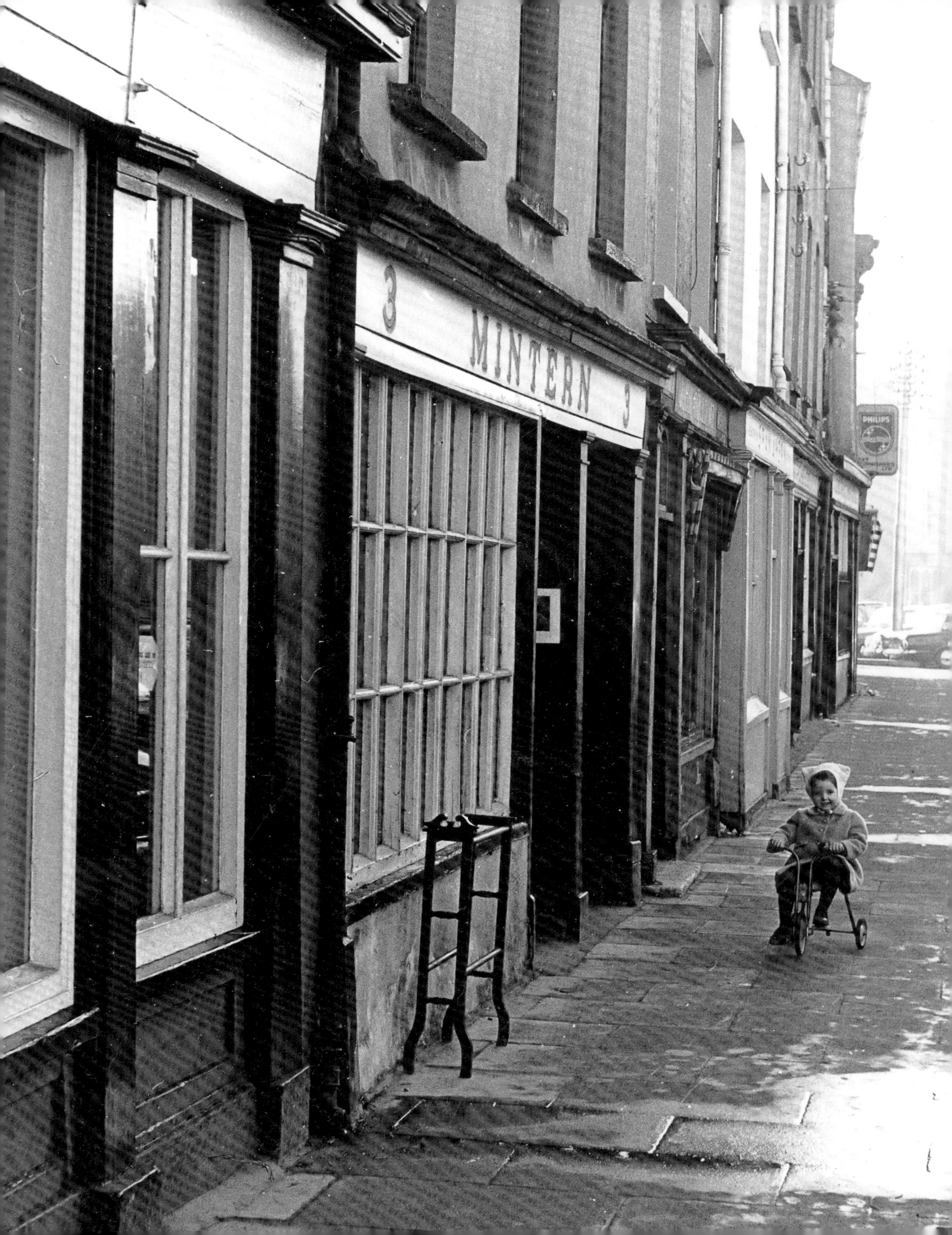
3
MINTERN
3
PHILIPS

Established in 1928 on Patrick's Quay, Woollams garage had seen better days when this picture was taken.

A sign of different times – many children in buggies were left alone outside shops. These two have had enough time to remove their shoes.

A woman admires her friend's children with their matching jackets. Their fashionable mother seems to have adopted the new beehive hairstyle. In the background the electrical shop RenTel was the distributor for General Electric Company products.

The heat in Kinsale on this day out appears to be having a soporific effect on day-trippers.

Above: These two well-dressed young girls on the Coal Quay are extremely interested in events going on behind the doorway. In the background a large trailer laden with boxes is making a delivery to Musgrave's wholesalers. The entrance to Little Cornmarket Street laneway is next to the lorry.

Right: A widow wearing the traditional black walks with a girl in a hand-knit Aran cardigan. They pass near Foley's shop in Patrick's Street, which was a stockist of souvenirs, confectionary and cigarettes, and also had a great selection of cigars.

101

The old telephone boxes, once a familiar sight on Patrick's Street, are long gone. It appears that the two hatted men inhabit a different climate zone to their fashionable young counterpart.

Patrick's Street was a great place to have your new motorbike examined by jealous onlookers. The CIÉ bus advertises Guinness 'One up, one down' as a Ford Anglia car pulls out.

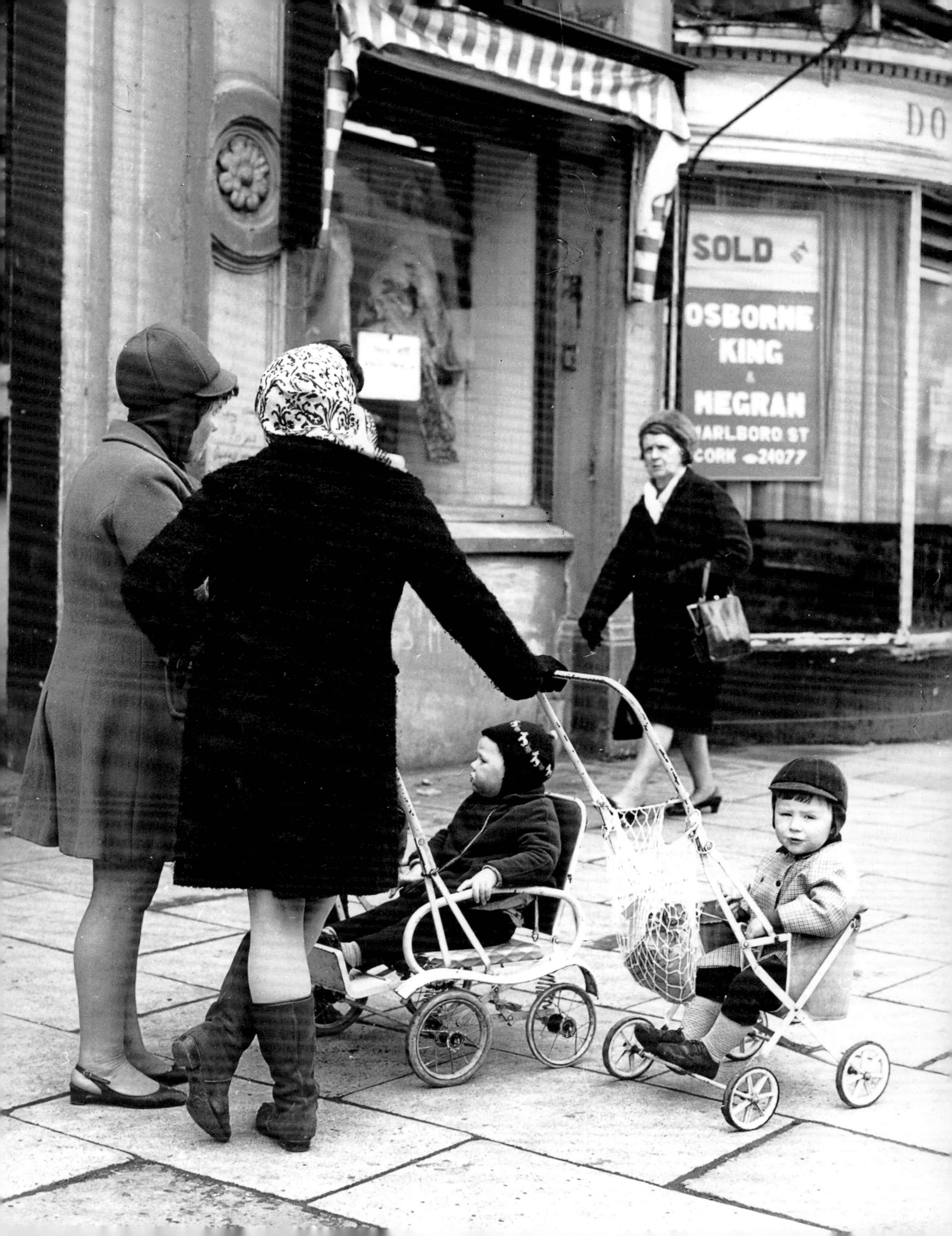
DO
SOLD
OSBORNE
KING
&
MEGRAN
MARLBORO ST
CORK 24077

Above: Uncharacteristically jovial businessmen cross the street.

Left: Two women chat outside the Grand Parade entrance of the English Market, while their children wait patiently in their go-cars.

Left: A boy carries his terrier under his arm outside a fruit shop on the Grand Parade. The mosaic tiles on the shop front were typical of their time. This photograph was taken at Eastertime, as there are Easter Eggs in the window display.

Above: A beautifully turned out family walks in front of Bolger's in Patrick's Street with its wonderful striped canopy.

Overleaf: A waiting crowd outside the Queens Old Castle on the Grand Parade are watching a St Patrick's Day parade passing by. One woman takes advantage of two concrete blocks to improve her view.

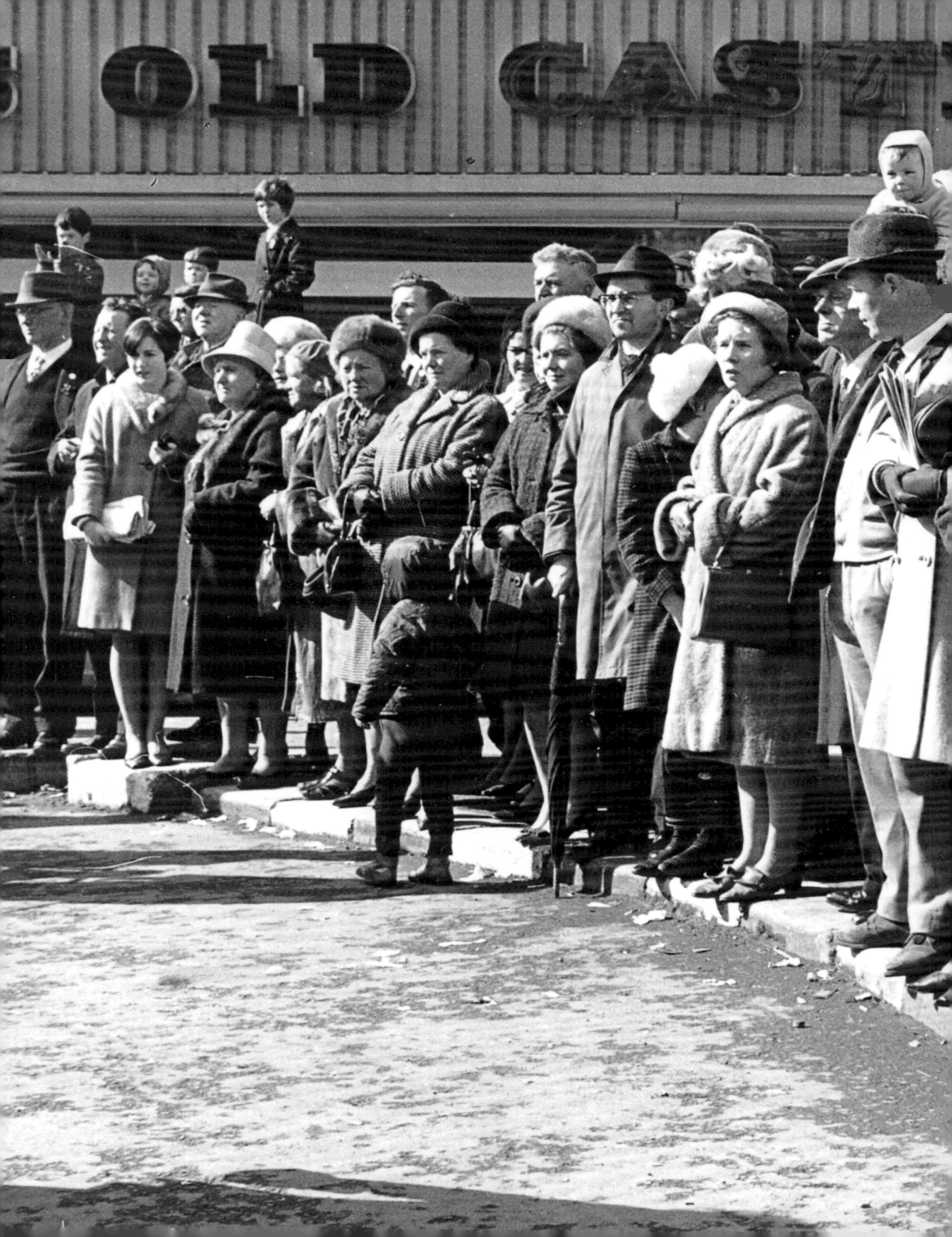
OLD CAST

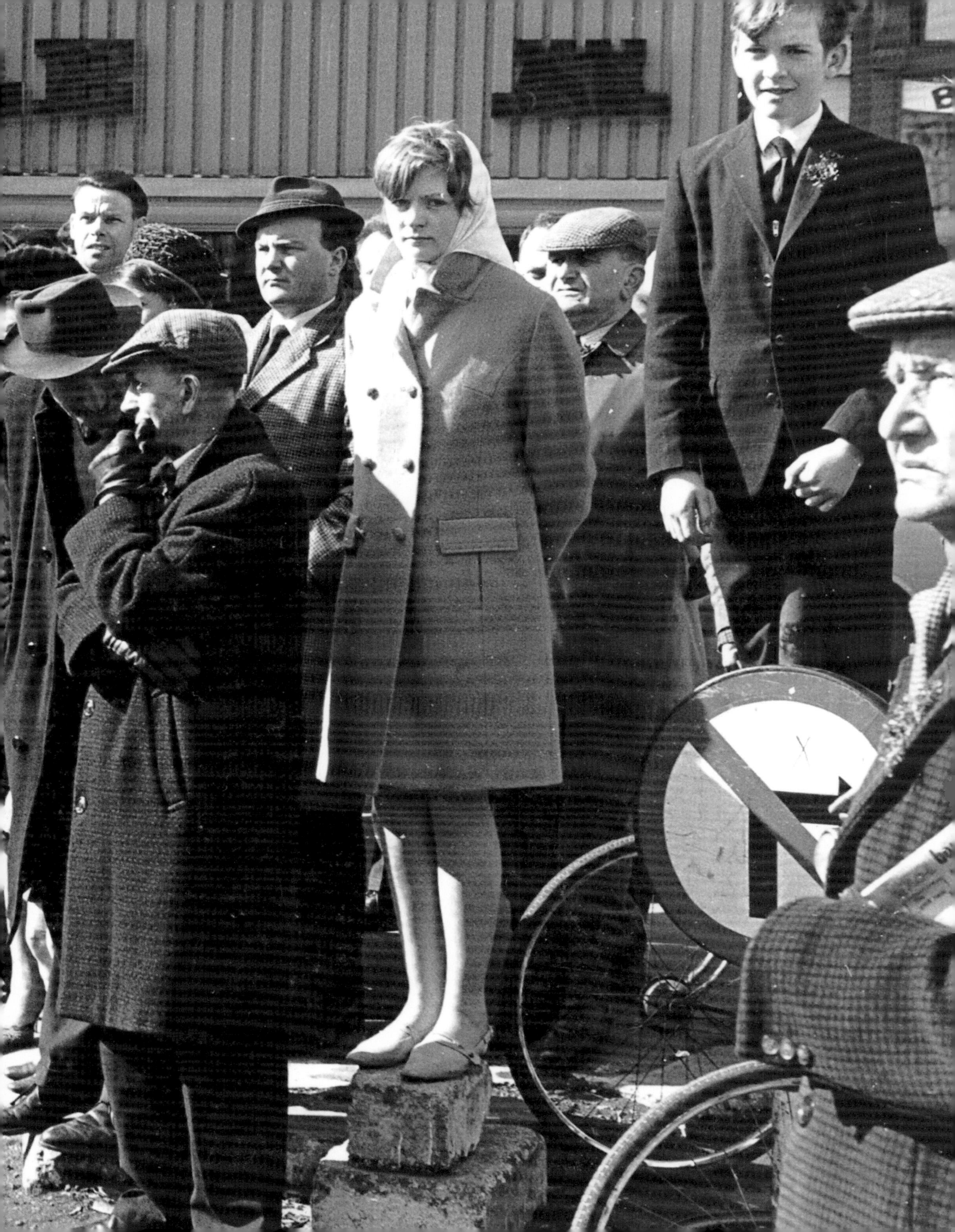

Above: Four women having a laugh are passing the steps at one of Cork's favourite cinemas, the Pavilion on Patrick's Street. Affectionately known as the Pav, it also had one of Cork's finest restaurants. The window of its confectionary shop displays an array of Black Magic, Quality Street, Dairy Milk and Smarties, as well as Tayto crisps at 4 pence per bag.

Top right: Shorter hem lengths and traditional head scarves are brought together by these trendy ladies preparing to cross the road outside Bolger's on Patrick's Street.

Bottom right: Note the lawnmower in the back of this Mercedes car parked outside Le Château, 93 Patrick's Street, one of the oldest licensed premises in the city .

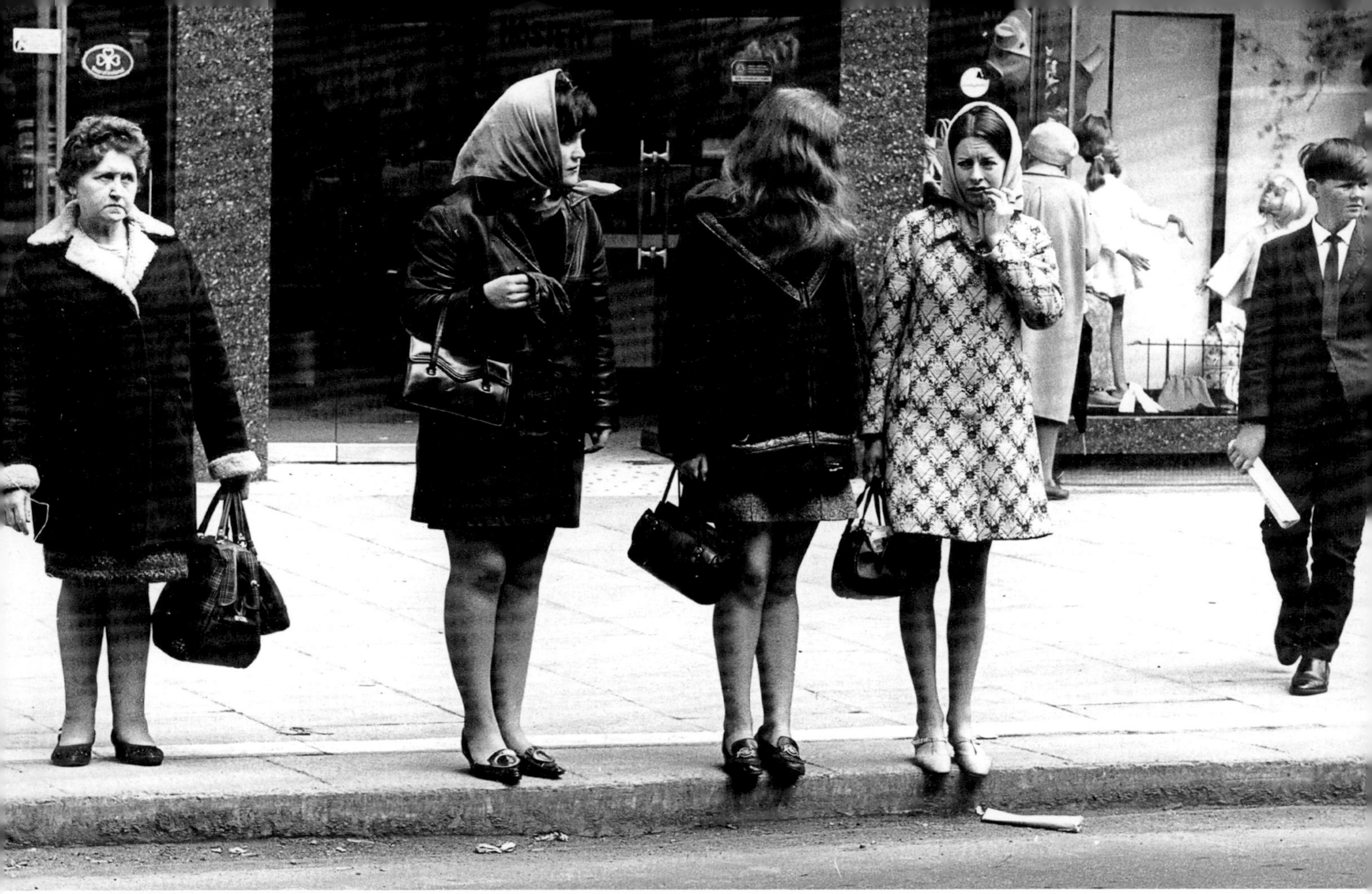

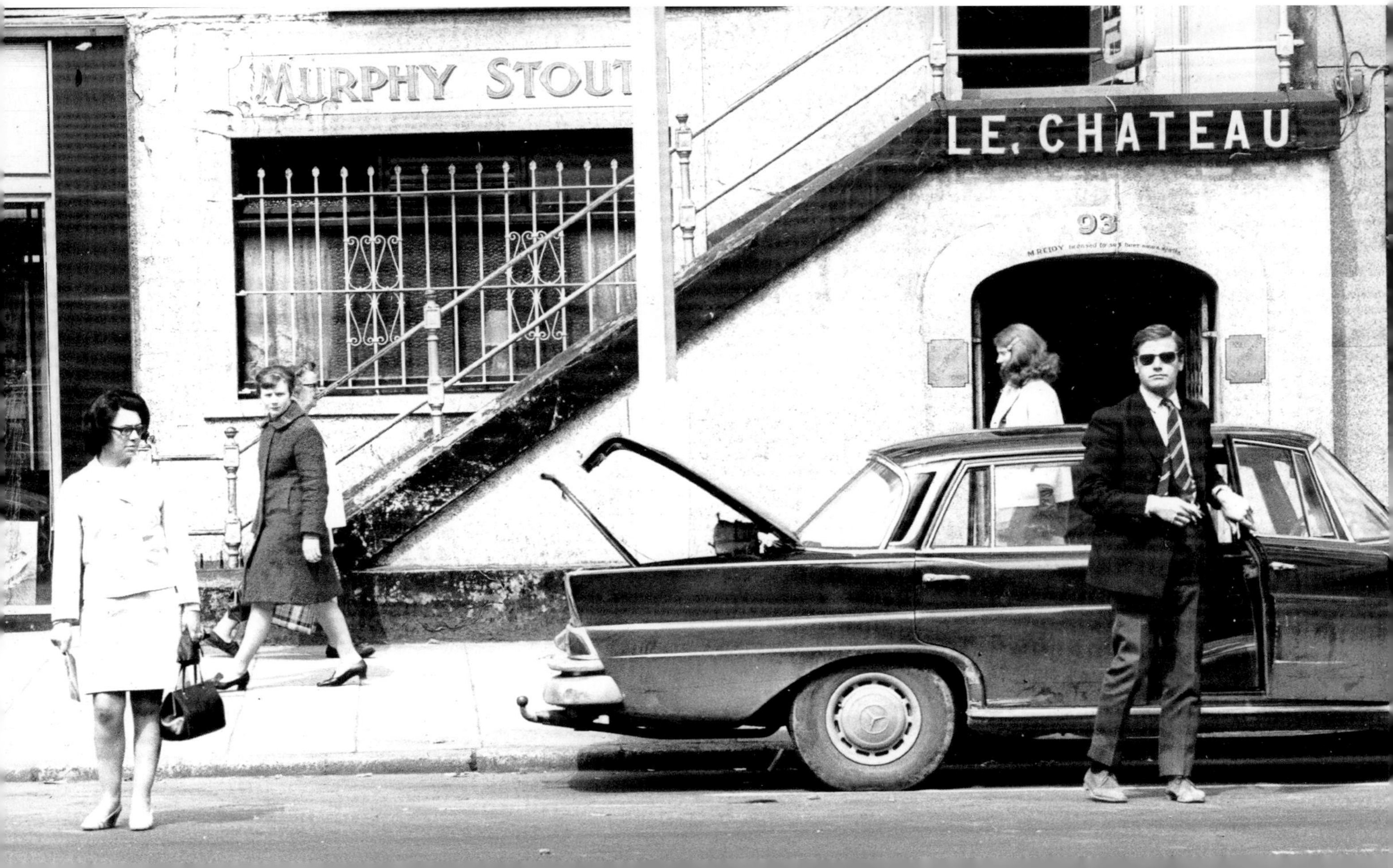
MURPHY STOUT
LE. CHATEAU
93

Although Patrick's Street was always busy with shoppers, people still had time to stop and talk. The talented banjo player Christy Dunne plays in the background.

A matriarchal figure has her trusty straw bag at the ready as she prepares to go shopping on Patrick's Street. A girl with her own miniature shopping basket is distracted from her mother's encounter by an ice cream, probably purchased from the nearby Woolworth's store.

Above: Changing fashions – the clothes the young men are wearing, as they hurry along near the RenTel electrical shop, are an indication of a more casual look that was just coming to the fore.

Right: A young girl digs with her shovel as the steeple of Shandon, Cork's most iconic building, towers behind on Eason's Hill.

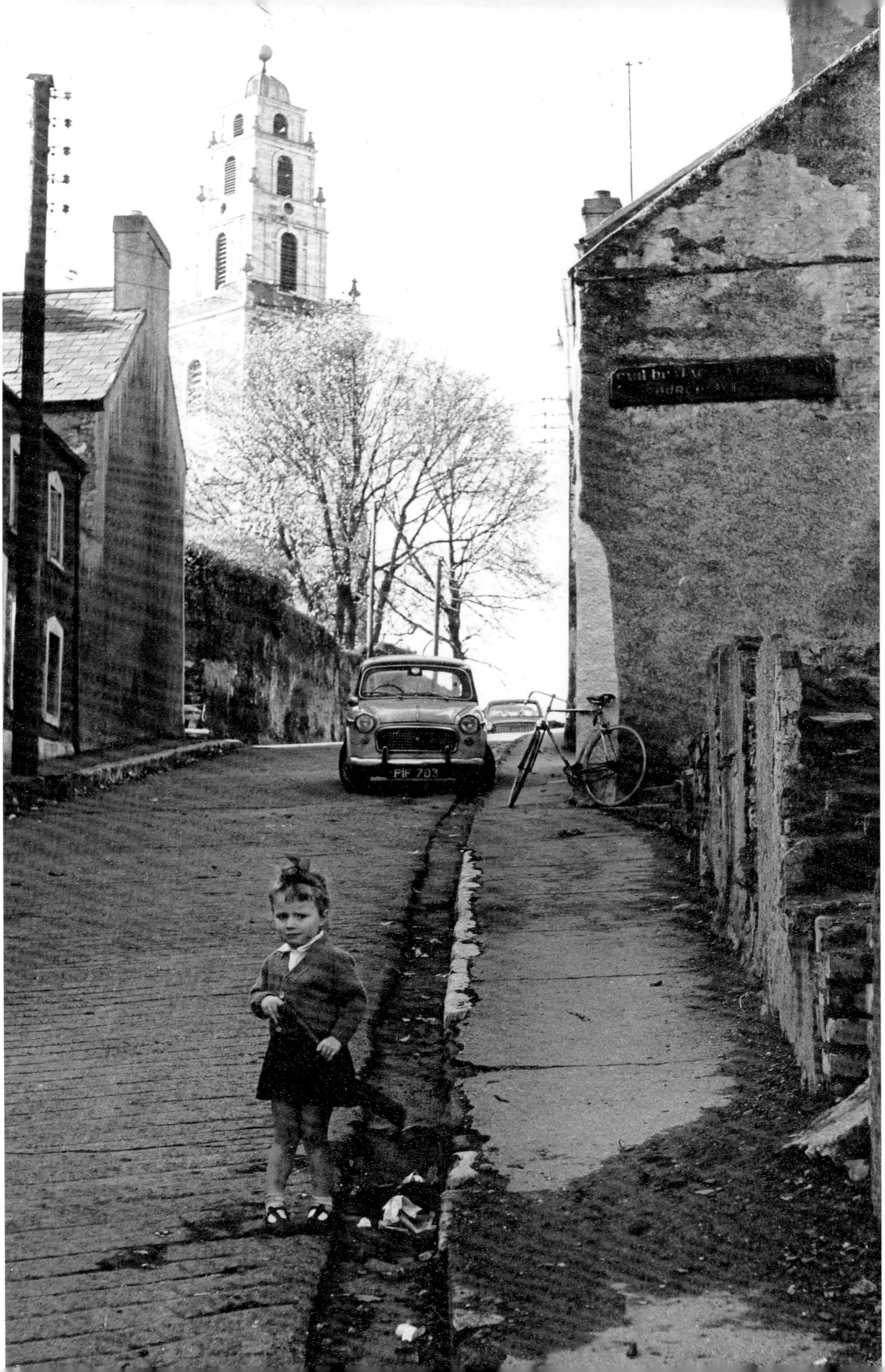
PIF 703

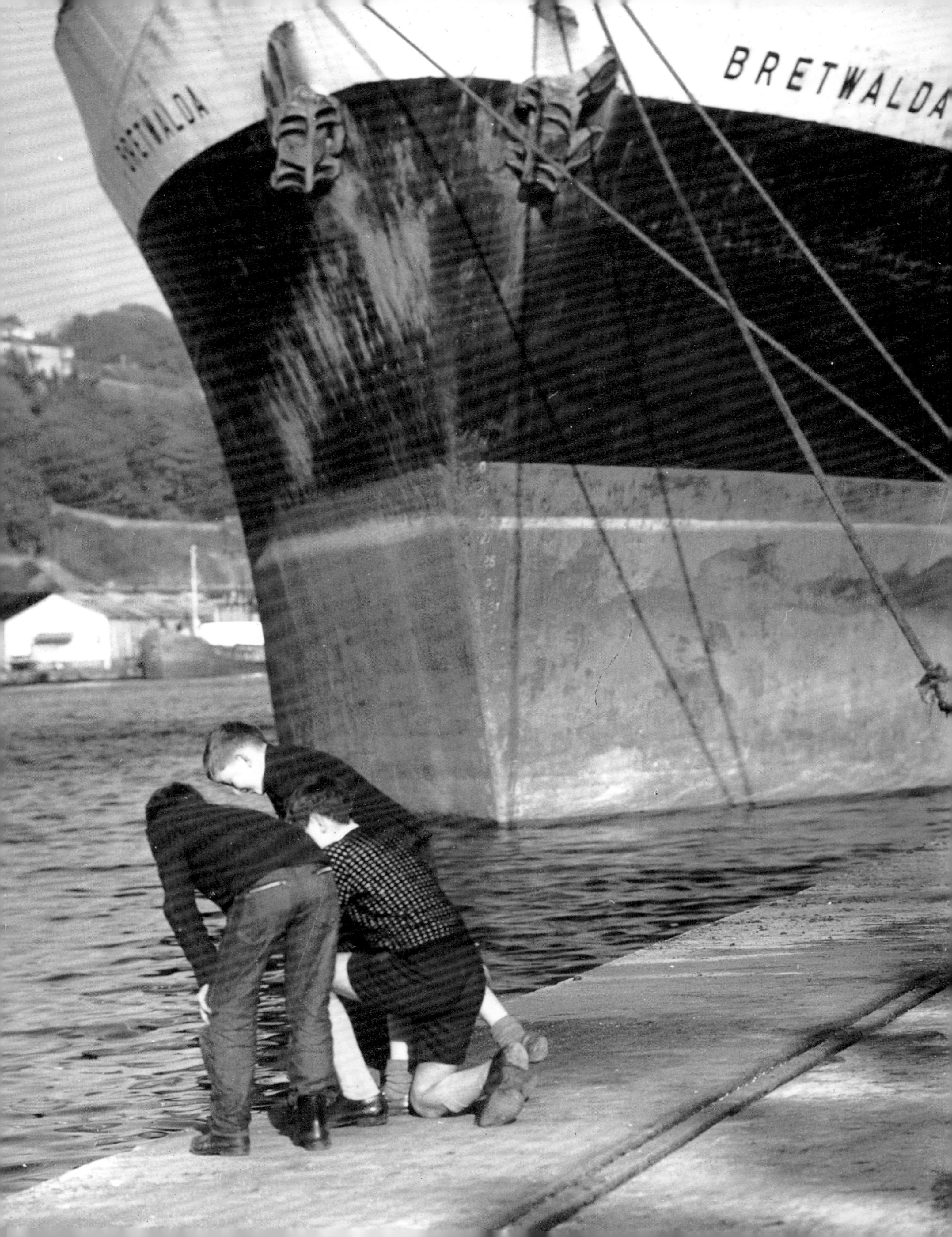
BRETWALDA
BRETWALDA

Above: The Telefusion television shop on Prince's Street, where you could rent your television for four shillings eleven pence complete with television licence. Television was still in its infancy as RTÉ, in black and white, was the only option available.

Left: The *Bretwalda*, just one of the very many ships that docked at Cork's Quays. The ship dwarfs the boys peering into the waters beneath.

Above: Two boys smiling happily on a quayside bench, flanked by a Ford Mark I Cortina and an Austin Cambridge.

Right: Two children playing on Keyser's Hill near St Fin Barre's cathedral. Keyser's Hill has one of the oldest names in the city, dating back to Viking times, and means 'the pathway that leads to the wharf'.

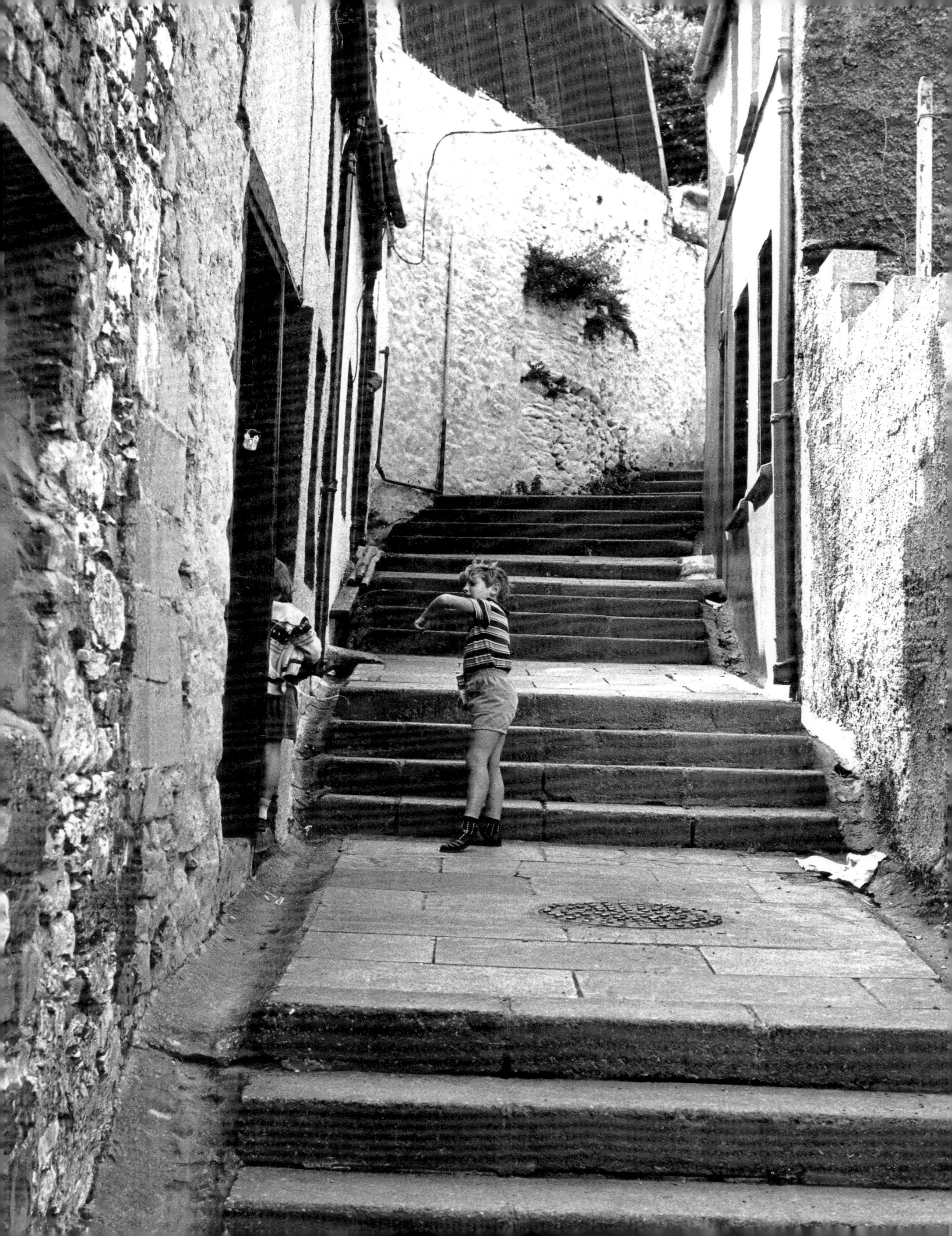

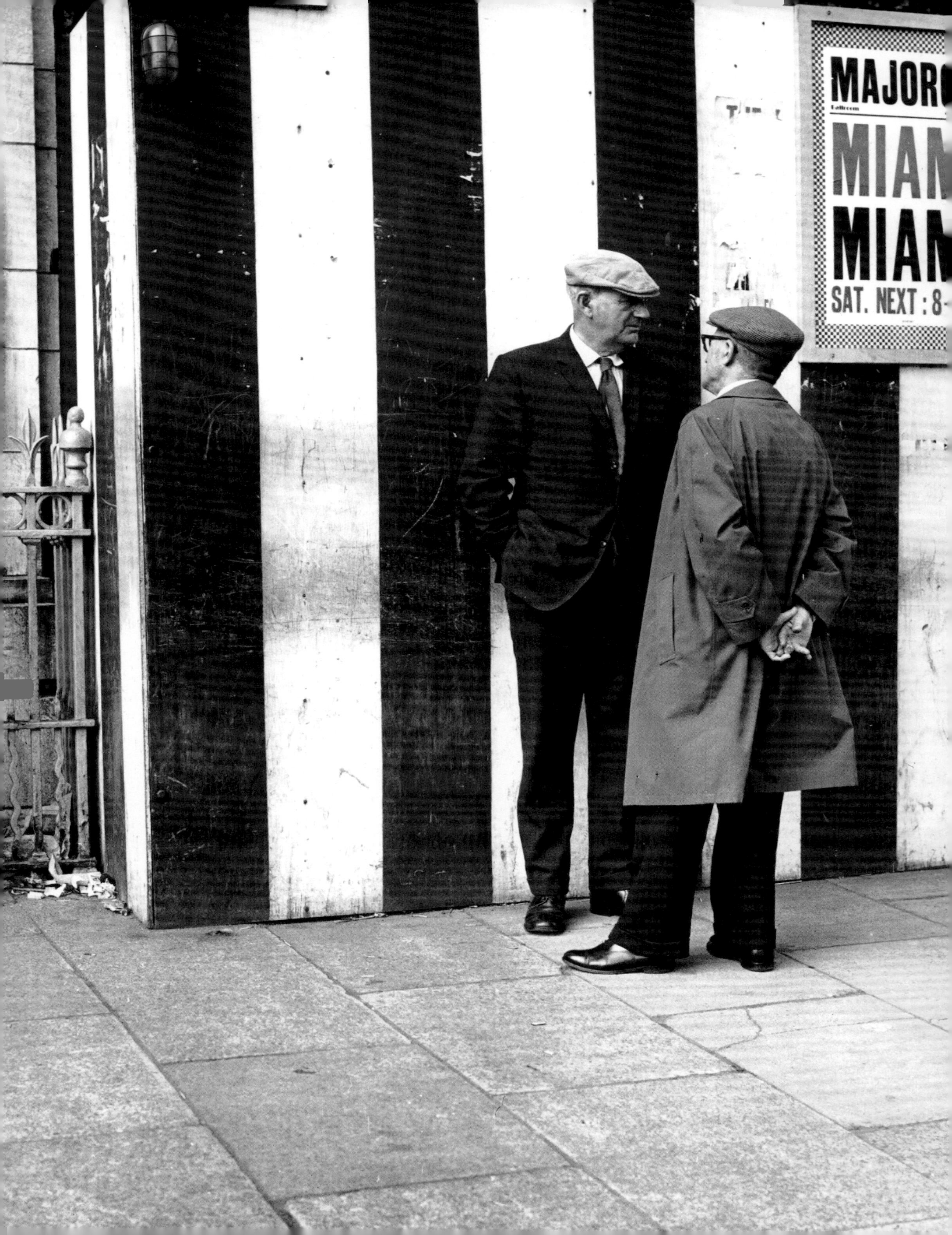
MAJOR
MIAM
MIAM
SAT. NEXT : 8

Above: Father and son, sporting matching haircuts, cross Patrick's Bridge as a musician busks.

Left: Two gentlemen talk beside a hoarding on the South Mall, to the left of the Hibernian buildings. The poster on the right advertises that the popular Miami showband were to appear at the Majorca dance hall in Crosshaven.

A judge at the Cork Summer Show admires two whippets. The Summer Show was one of the highlights of the agricultural calendar.

Above: Two flat-capped men enjoy the sweltering sunshine at the Cork Summer Show.

Right: In contrast, Diarmuid Barry, the photographer's grandson, is well prepared for rainy weather.

A good place to stop for a chat – on the wide footpath outside Woolworth's on Patrick's Street. The child in the go-car is holding on to a Roches Stores bag.

A well-dressed family wait to cross the road at the bottom of Bridge Street. Fitzgerald's familiar black and white chequered Morris 1000 van is heading towards its bakery, which was then located at 6 Coburg Street.

Above: A busy Fitzgerald's Park scene as the figures in the sculpture by Oisín Kelly look skywards. Affectionately known as Cha and Miah, these two Cork characters were made famous on RTÉ's *Hall's Pictorial Weekly*. They are now located outside the County Hall.

Right: A young girl with her double-breasted coat admires the fashions in the window of one of Cork's department stores. The display consists of ladies night attire and nylon stockings at two shillings and three pence, which were probably made at the Sunbeam factory in Blackpool.

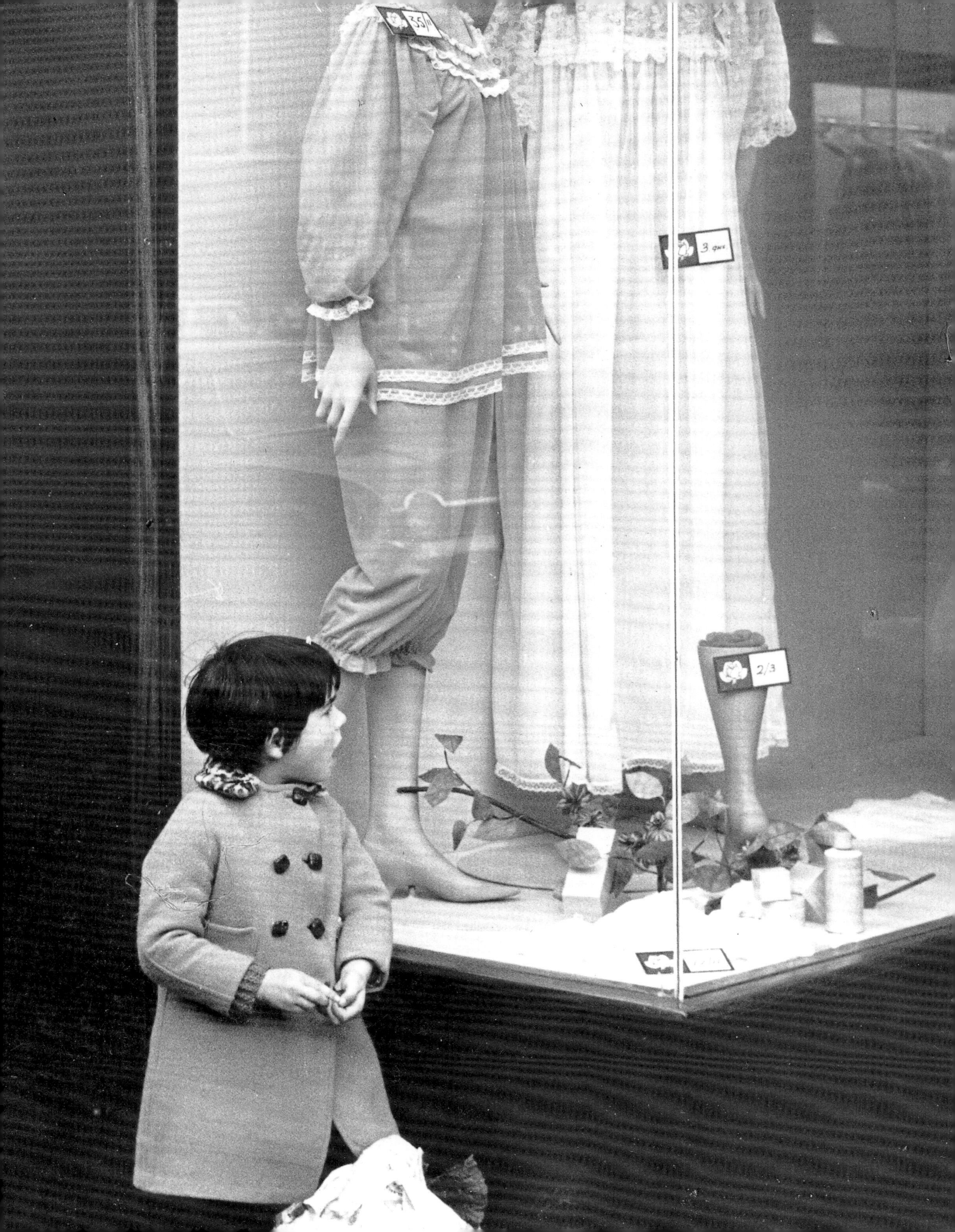
35/11
3 gns
2/3

A girl in her first communion dress about to board one of the old double-decker buses. The slogan on the bus – 'Save the tiger' – refers to Esso's saving stamp campaign.

A great crowd looking for a bargain gathers outside J. Busteed's mattress-makers store on the Coal Quay. The laneway to the left is Cock Pit Lane, one of the city's old medieval laneways.

Kellogg's
CORN FLAKES
Kellogg's
CORN FLAKES

KODACHROME COLOUR FILM
Kodak FILM
DEVELOPING PRINTING ENLARGING
ILFORD
Films

Above: A boy sits on the steps of Guinness House, Patrick's Street, enjoying a banana, as he minds the shopping.

Left: Two men lean on the window sill of a shop selling Kodak and Ilford film, enjoying the sunshine.

Standing in a doorway in front of an office door adorned with letter boxes at Moloney's Solicitors, 70 South Mall. The woman to the right is clutching her messages and her Cassidy's fashion store shopping bag.

A bangharda and her superior have a discussion. Banghardaí were still a rare sight in the early 1960s. In the background are a Ford Cortina Mark II and an Austin A40.

This family outing into the city included the dog. John O'Donovan, his son Tim and daughter Sharon stand on the roadway to cross the street, a less perilous occupation in those days. To the rear the different forms of transport include a Ford Corsair, Mini, Cortina Mark I and a Volkswagen van.

Outside Eason's on Patrick's Street a woman writes a postcard as a man reads a paper and a boy reads his comic.

For many years this fruit seller, Mamie Murphy, sold her fruit at Camden Quay. This location had very good passing trade as it was close to St Mary's church on Pope's Quay.

The popular Leprechaun restaurant and cafe was located just around the corner from Foley's confectioners shop at 101 Patrick's Street. The first parked car is a Morris Minor, affectionately known as a galloping maggot because of its shape.

Two gardaí on the beat outside John Cronin's menswear, 59 Oliver Plunkett Street. The new garda uniform was introduced in 1952. No. 58, Macroom Dairies, later became the Farmhouse cake shop and restaurant.

Two women consider the fashions with great intensity in this shop window on Prince's Street.

Above: The Transport Warehousing Co.'s Commer truck provides the backdrop for these two men who have stopped to have a chat. Parked in the background is a Ford Prefect, while a Ford Cortina Mark I passes by.

Right: Angela Walsh is the Coal Quay dealer smoking a cigarette as she looks on at the bargain hunters near the Bridewell garda station.

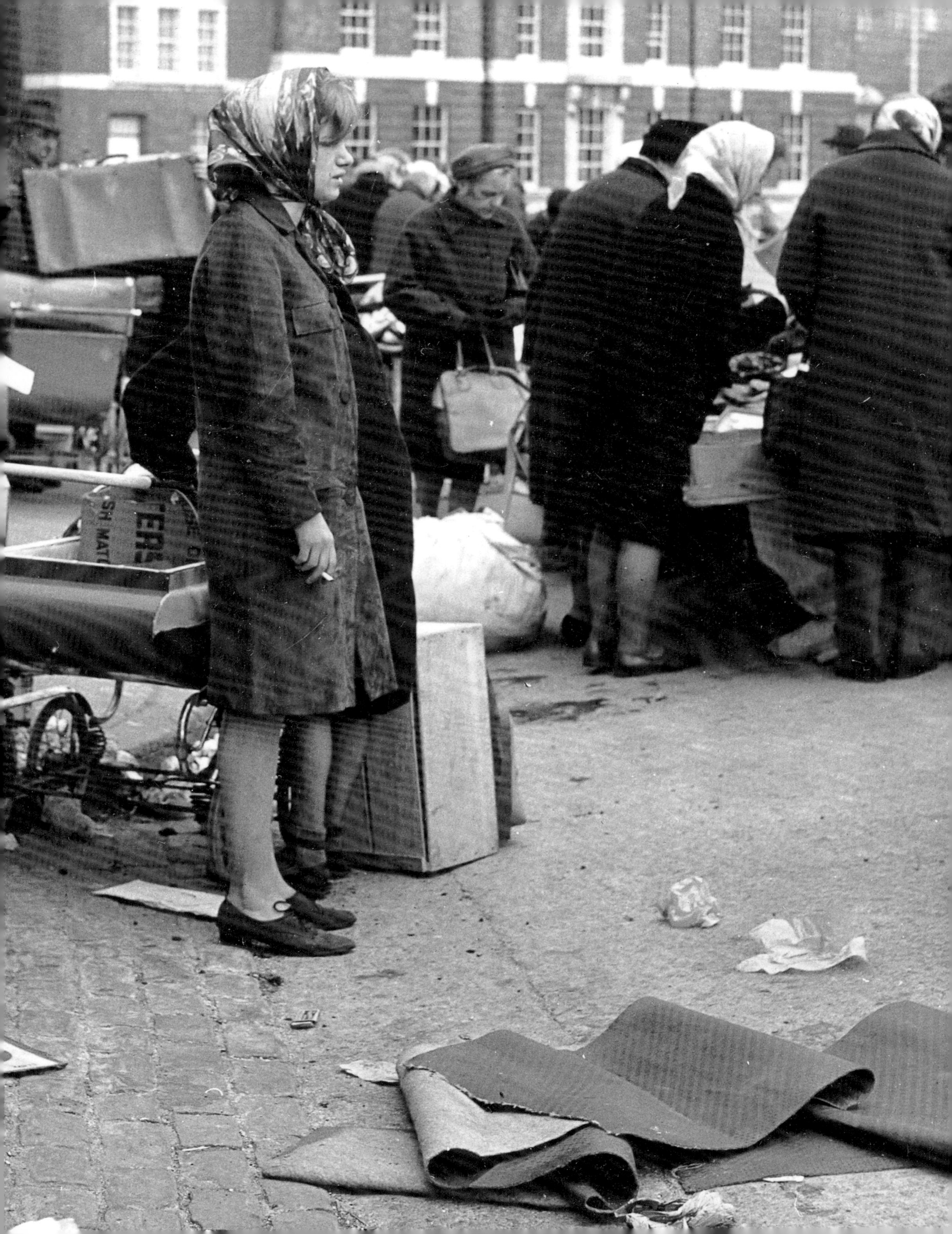

Jackson's Furniture Stores at 55 Cornmarket Street, where new and second-hand furniture was bought and sold. Unfortunately this premises closed in April 2014, after years of service on the Coal Quay.

The candy-striped Queens Old Castle Bedford van on Academy Street. Their store on the Grand Parade opened in 1846 and specialised in drapery and home furnishings.

John Roche Ltd carried not only a huge selection of fishing equipment and tackle, but their range of toy cars was second to none. Big brand names such as Corgi, Dinky and Matchbox were always on display in the shop window.

A Ford Anglia passes the top of Cook Street as the girl in the polka dot dress checks her purse for change. The two girls waiting to cross the road wear matching dresses.

A man looks on as a bangharda passes T. W. Murray's sports shop at 87 Patrick's Street. This shop has been providing fishing and sports equipment to generations of Cork citizens since 1828.

A horse and covered cart driven by Mikey O'Donovan belonging to A. Buckley's of Lavitt's Quay makes its way down Paul Street. To the right cars and vans have been parked haphazardly on the street and footpath.

The House of Cassidy's banners proclaim their summer sale, as the customary go-cars are left outside while mother shops inside.

The steps by Morrogh's stockbrokers (est. 1897) at 74 South Mall remind us that this street was once a waterway.

Vegetable seller Nellie Brady amongst the rickety makeshift tables and wooden boxes which she used to display her wares on the Coal Quay.

There always seemed to be more activity outside than inside Twomey's shop at the top of the Coal Quay. To the left was Browne's wholesale sweet and tobacco store.

The occupant of this pram is being admired by a matriarchal woman, at a time when these sturdy well-sprung conveyances were the order of the day. The Togher bus advertises Lucas Electrical Equipment, which was located on Bachelor's Quay and specialised in auto electrical parts, dynamos, starter motors, car batteries and headlights.

Right: A conversation outside the dry cleaners on Patrick's Street. During the 1960s a plethora of dry cleaning companies such as Antoine, IMCO, McKechnie's and Prescott's opened for business in the city.

Below: A man passes the offices of S. J. Murphy & Co., a shipping and forwarding business in Parnell Place.

Above: White Heather Taxis were often parked in the taxi rank on Patrick's Street. In the background is an old Honda 175 motorcycle. The taxi is a Ford Zephyr, which was a very luxurious model at the time.

Right: Two old friends clasp hands outside the Moderne on Patrick's Street, which has only recently relocated. Many a courting Cork couple met outside this boutique on their first date.

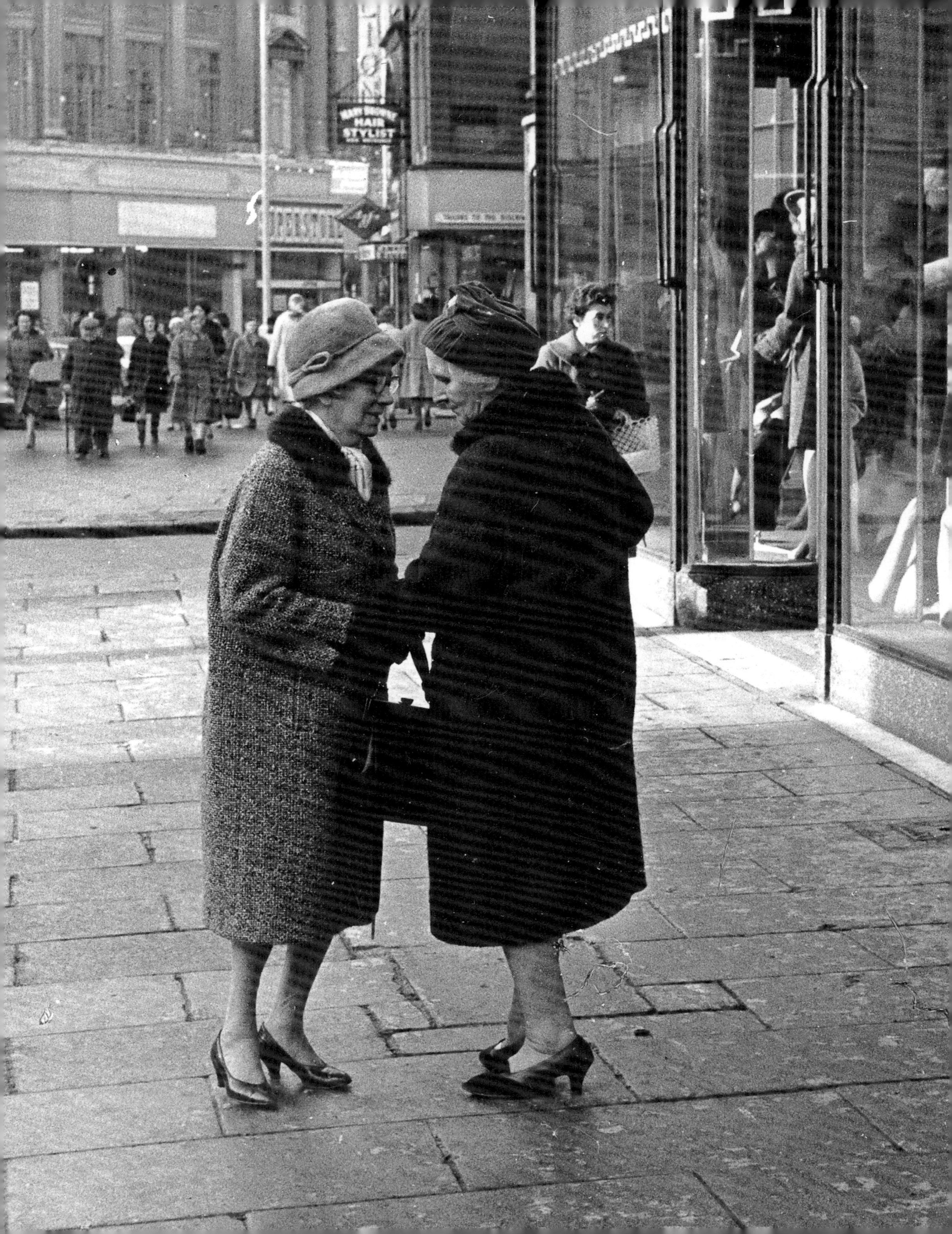
HAIR
STYLIST

Above: A busy street scene at the top of Academy Street, leading on to Patrick's Street. A workman has his ladder perched outside McSweeney's chemists, 91 Patrick's Street.

Right: Two ladies in sheepskin coats outside the old Cork library established in 1792. The owls on the outside are believed to have been carved by the famous Cork sculptor John Hogan. The old library was located on the corner of South Mall and Pembroke Street and this entrance was on the latter.

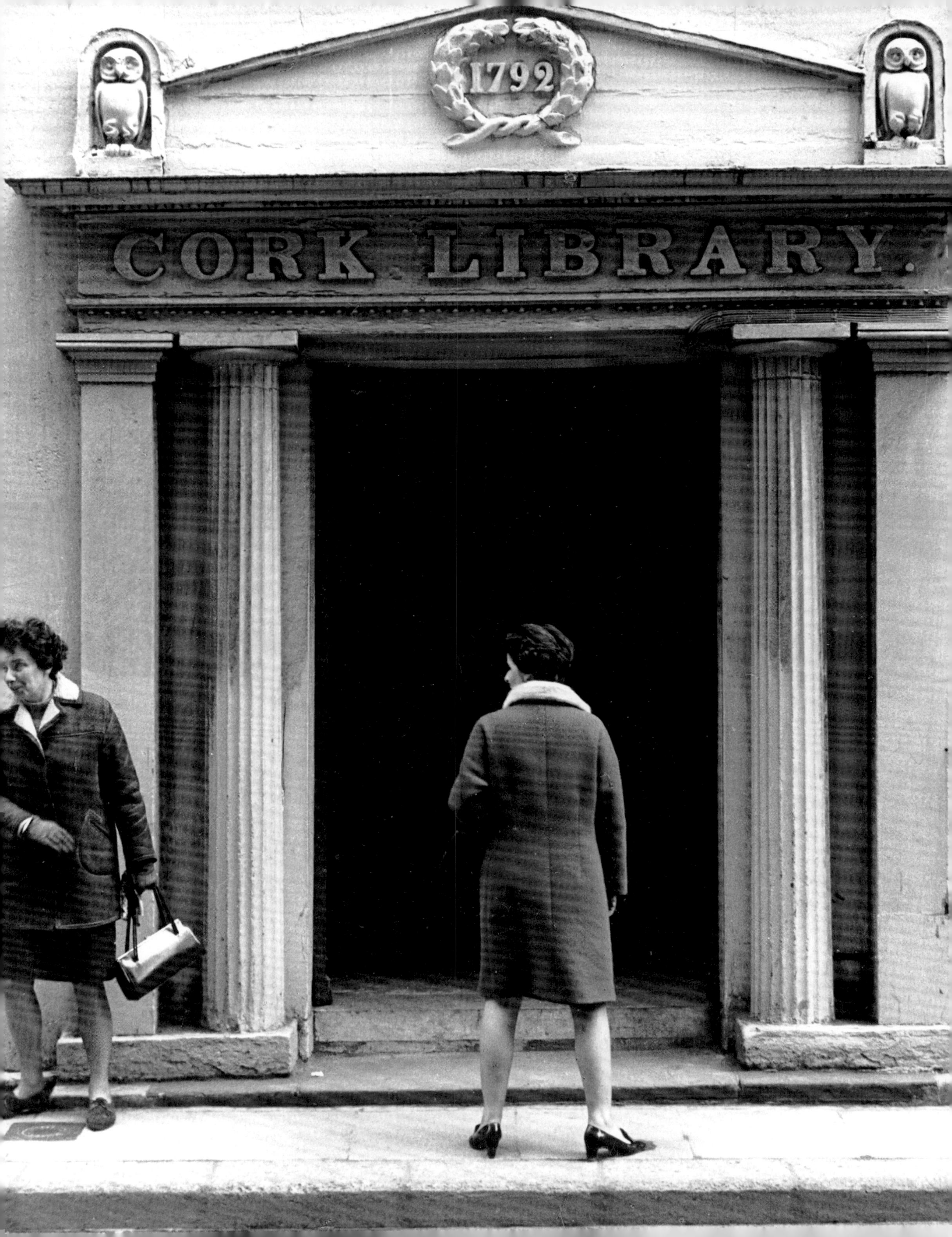
1792
CORK LIBRARY.

Punch was a name synonymous with the Coal Quay, as generations of this family traded there. The sign advertising Clarke's plug tobacco was for the nearby factory on Lavitt's Quay. To the left is Blackie the dog, Pat Punch sits on the table (*right*) and sitting facing the camera is Annie Punch.

Even in the inner city fishing was a popular pastime, as these boys fishing from a pontoon (probably in Blackrock) clearly demonstrate.

Above: A mad rush to board the bus outside Barry & Hyland's footwear shop on Patrick's Street. The advertising sign on the bus states 'Come alive, you're in the Pepsi generation'.

Right: The *Echo* boy sorts out change for a customer, as he displays his papers on the pavement. Fortunately the newspaper sellers are still a familiar sight on the streets of Cork, although they are not quite as young any more.

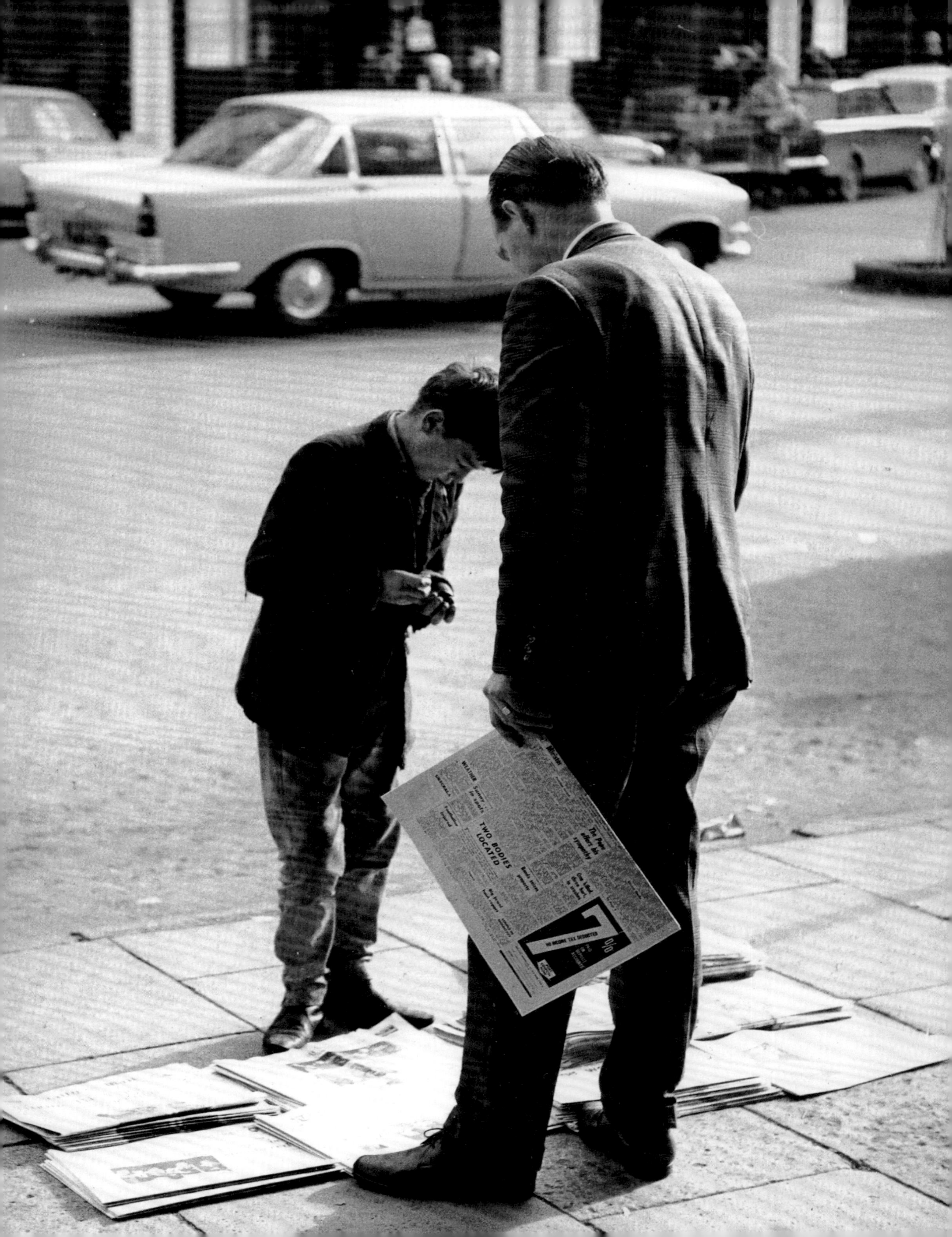
WEATHER
TWO BODIES LOCATED
7%

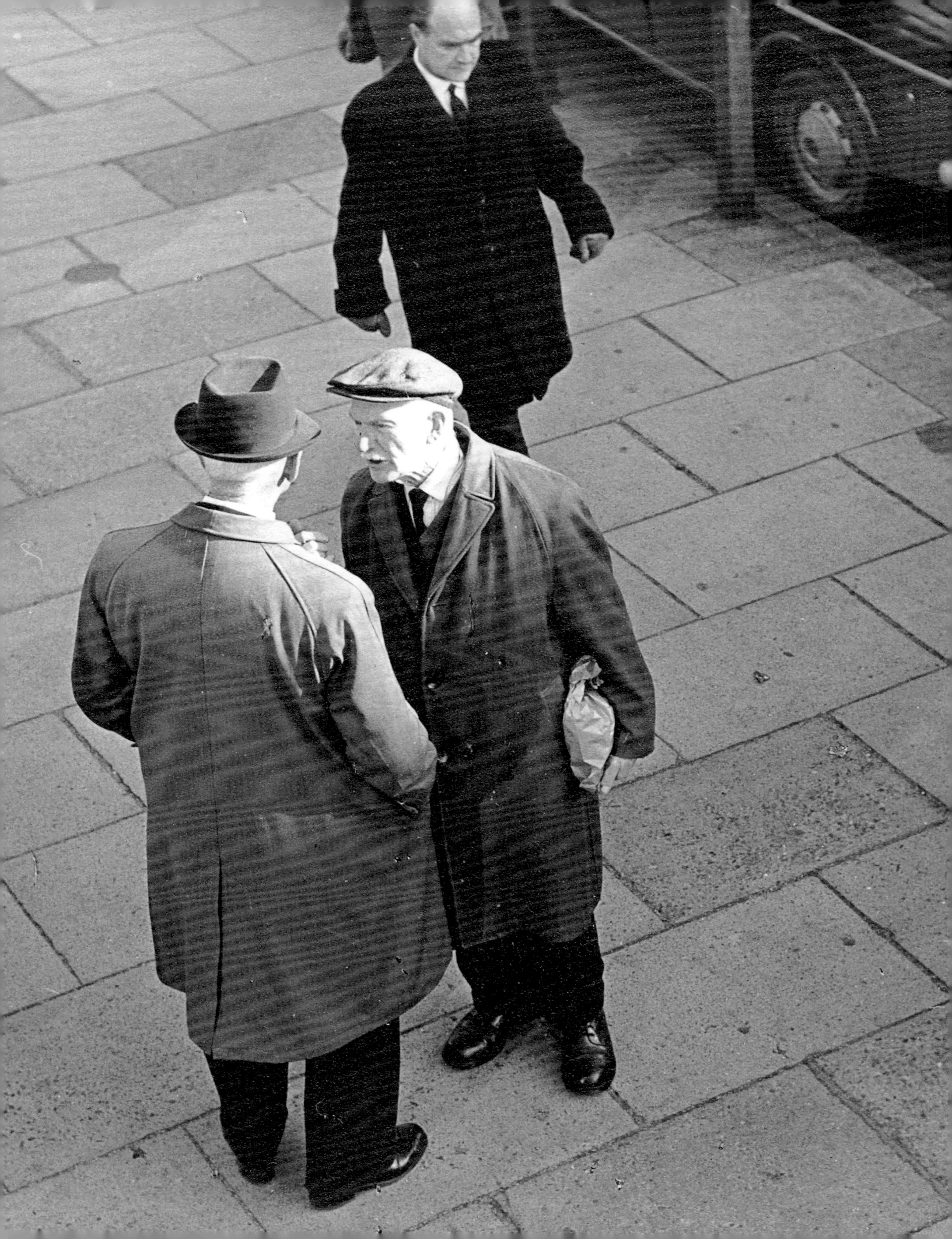

Above: Outside one of Cork's oldest businesses, Woodford Bourne's. Their main products were wines, spirits and bottled beers, and they had a huge bonded stores on Sheare's Street. They also sold tea, fruit and flowers.

Left: A very serious conversation takes place.

Bolger's department store on Patrick's Street displays the very latest summer wear. Cudmore's, which sold fresh fruit, ice cream, cigarettes, sweets and chocolates, had one of their branches directly opposite.

A busy scene with prospective customers and pedestrians intermingling near an old arched doorway on the Coal Quay. The dealer in the centre facing the camera is Jenny Rahilly.

Above: Cork palates are educated in the latest in world cuisine: Chinese food from the Tung Sun and Italian from Lo Zio Pino on Washington Street.

Right: McKenzies on Camden Quay, established in 1876, was an agricultural suppliers, stocking shovels, spades, animal feed and the latest agricultural machinery. This building was in use until recently as a temporary courthouse.

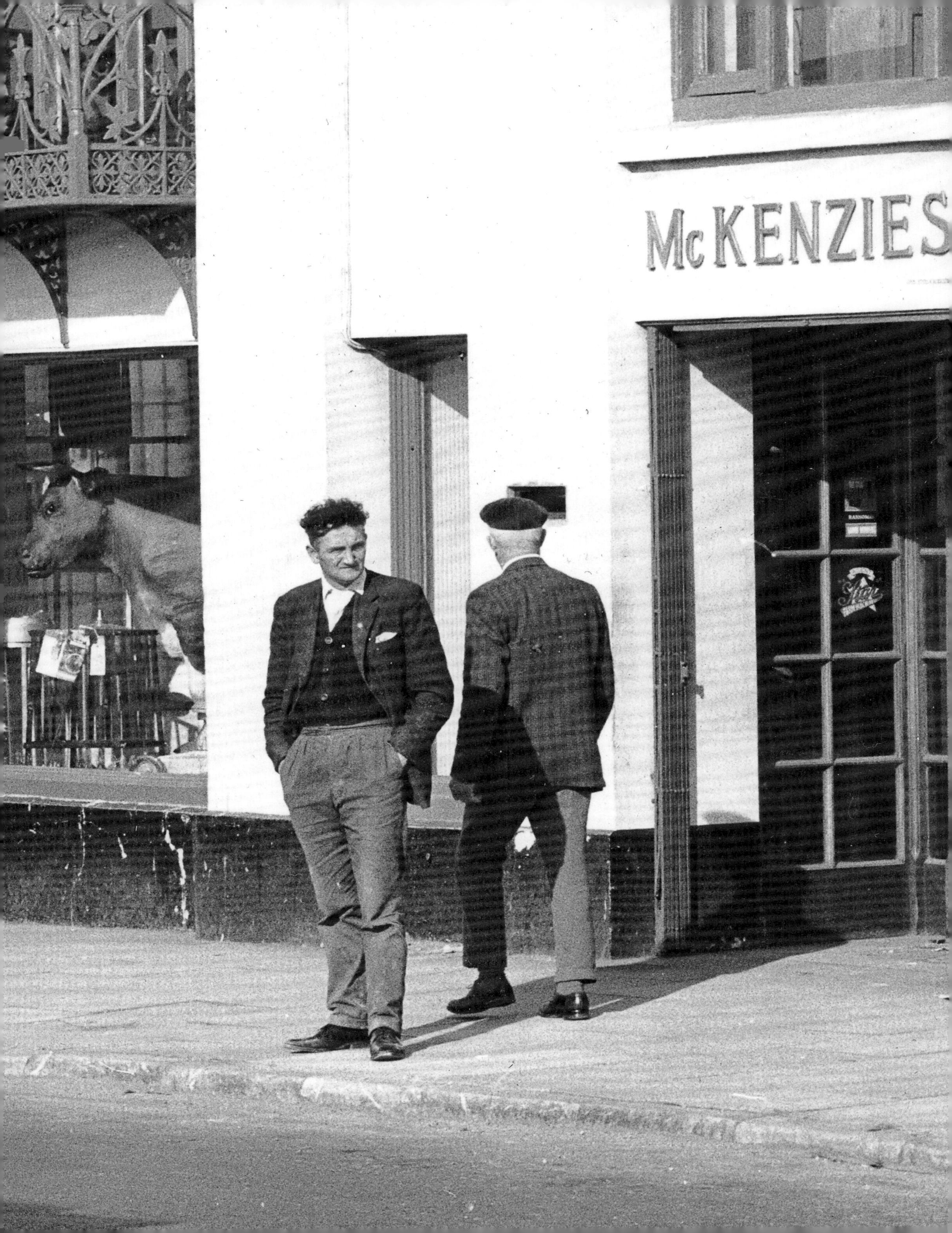
McKENZIES

Above: This photograph was taken during repair work on the Clontarf railway bridge. On 3 November 1965 the 1200 ton *City of Cork* cargo ship collided with the bridge, weakening the main supporting girder.

Right: A Cocker Spaniel takes a rest as his owner chats on Patrick's Street.

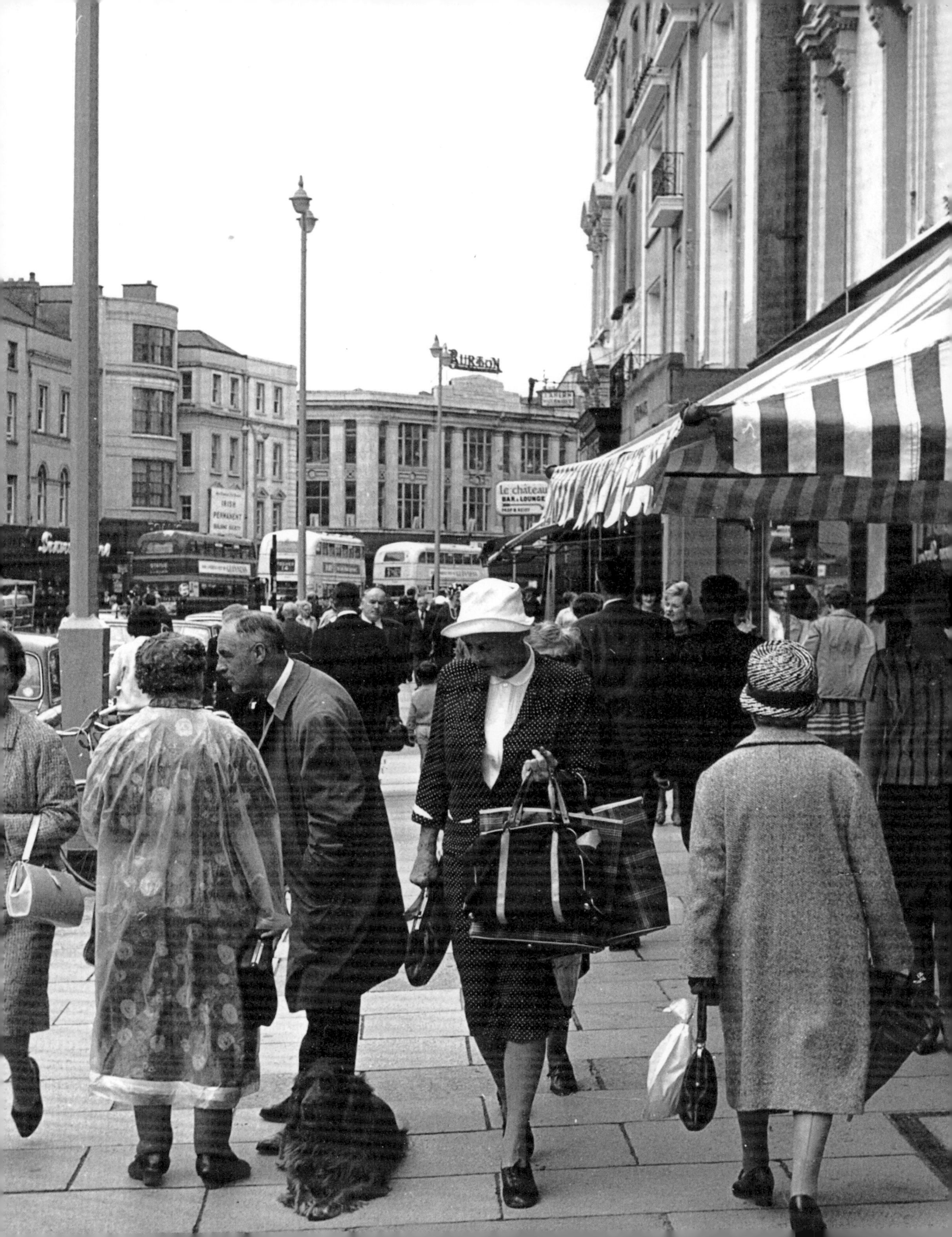
BURTON
IRISH
PERMANENT
le château
BAR & LOUNGE

A wonderful display at an open-air fruit and vegetable stall, near the entrance to the fish section of the English market, which was advertised as the New Market.

Boys fishing from the new Griffith Bridge, constructed in 1964 to replace the old wrought-iron North Gate Bridge which had been on this site for over 100 years. The old bridge had to be replaced as it could no longer cope with the volume of modern traffic.

IRISH
PERMANENT
ARCADIA
THE EXCITING!
COLLEGE
BOYS
SAT. DEC. 17
8-1
76

Renovation work going on behind the hoarding at the Irish Permanent Building Society office, 46 Patrick's Street.

Falvey's chemist on the corner of Bridge Street and Coburg Street. O'Connor's sign advertises car rentals. Their slogan was 'the right car at the right price'.

An old gentleman with a walking stick makes his way past Woolworth's on Patrick's Street as a pedestrian with her suitcases leans on the front façade.

A motley collection of clothes on a makeshift table – but no sign of any potential customers. It's time for a tea break outside this doorway and block wall on the Coal Quay.

A pram, tea chests and clothes on coat hangers on the wall are just part of this very dishevelled-looking open-air Coal Quay business.

An extremely long bus queue outside Cavendish's which advertises their hire purchase scheme. To the right is Burton's tailors – the highest compliment a man could be paid was 'you are like something out of Burton's window'.

The steps of the Fr Mathew statue were very handy for having a rest, or parking a bicycle. The statue was erected during the mayoralty of John Francis Maguire, MP, who also founded the *Cork Examiner* in 1841.

Above: Taking in a delivery near an old Fiat 500 car outside Woolworth's on Patrick's Street. The advertising sign on the litter bin for Tele-rents, 38 Prince's Street, states that they are 'Clearly the Best'.

Right: A messenger boy's bike is parked by the footpath as three friends stop for a chat outside a ladies' fashion shop on Patrick's Street.

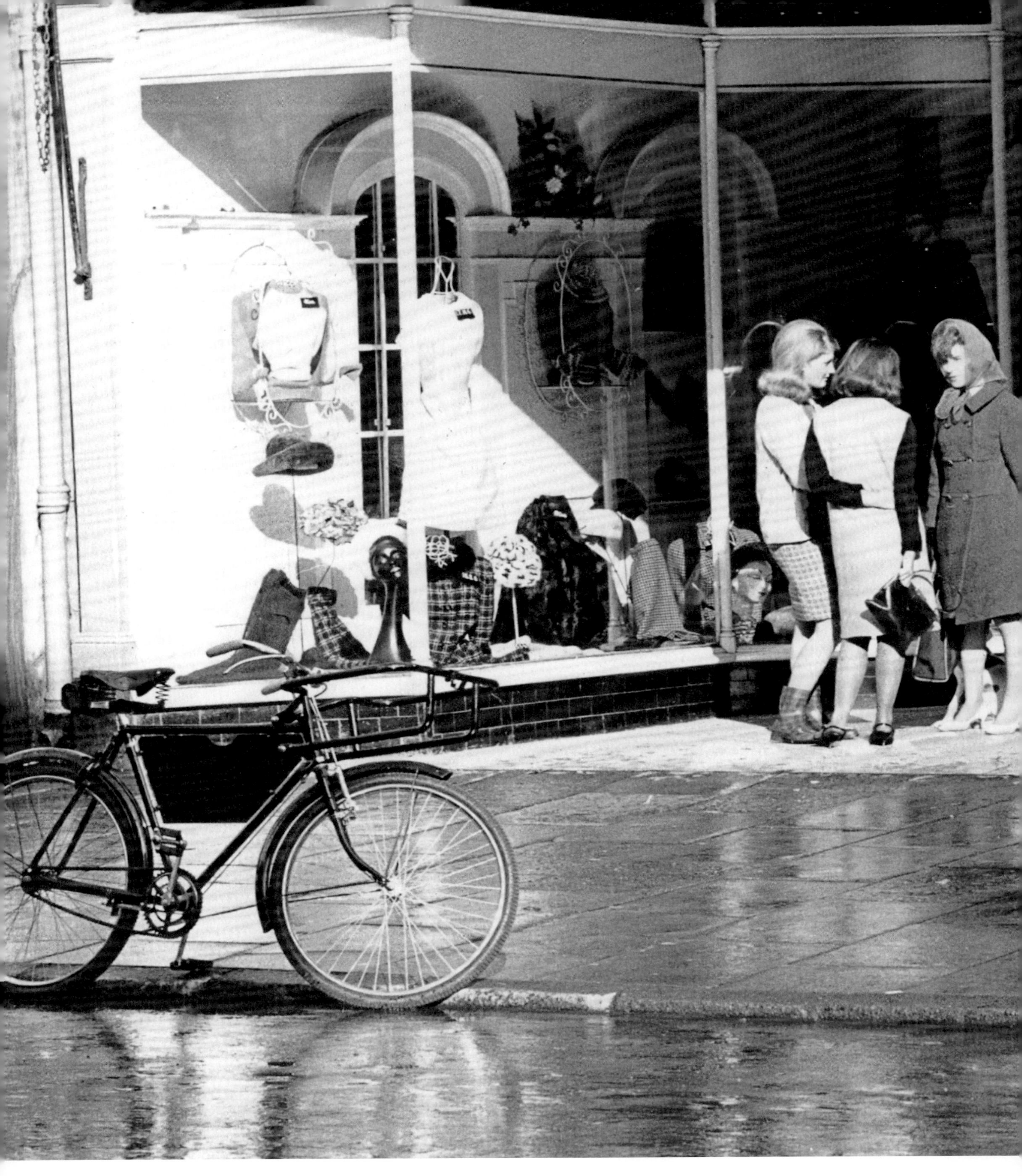

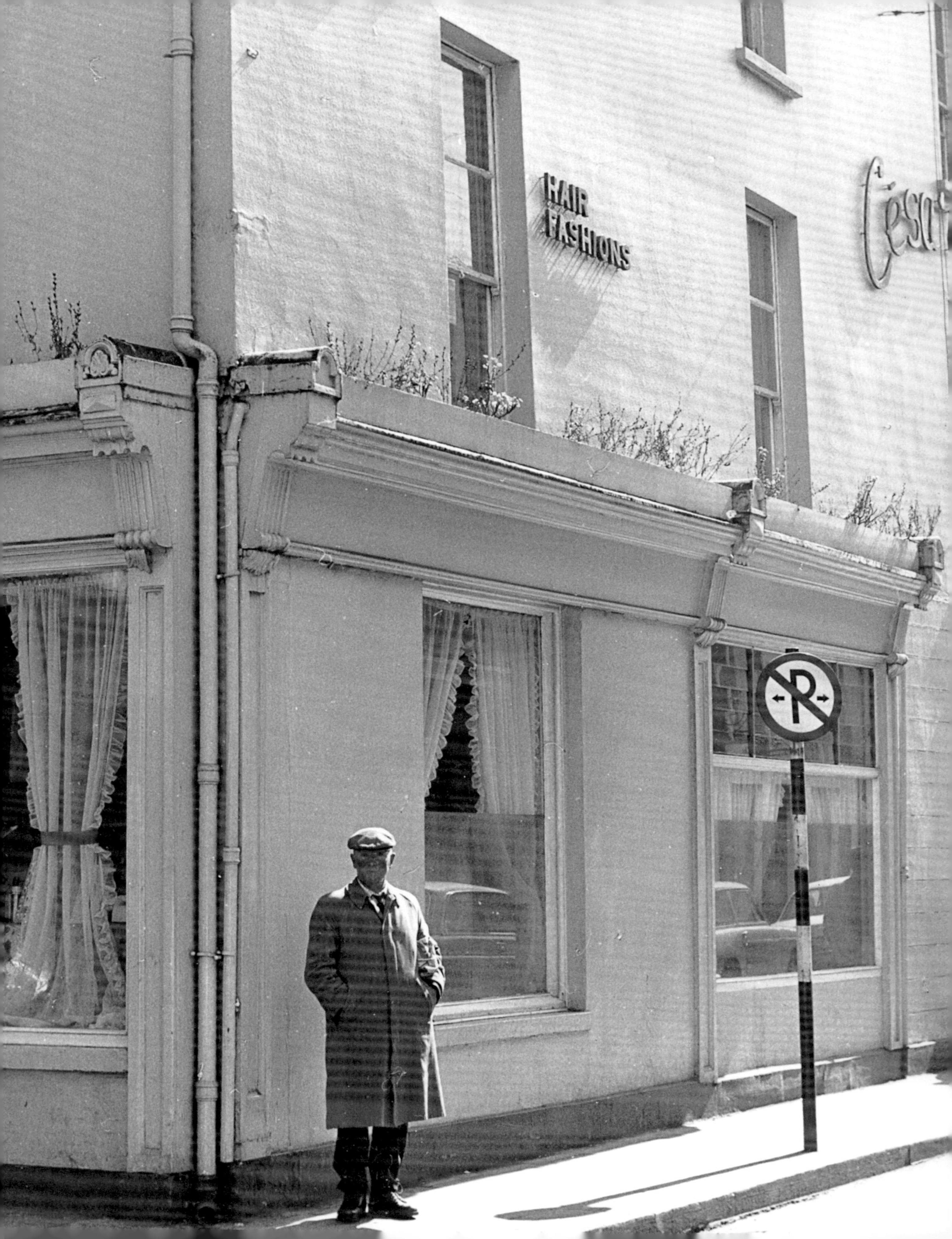
HAIR
FASHIONS

Above: Wearing a real fur coat. These could be purchased from Cork's well-known furriers Rohu, established in 1876, and Mockler's, where the best furs could cost as much as 375 guineas – the price of a motor car at the time.

Left: No parking outside César's hair fashions at 40 Oliver Plunkett Street – just one of the many stylists providing the very latest in London haircuts.

Above: A bangharda directs traffic near the Pavilion cinema. A colleague at the time, Garda Arthur O'Keeffe, was well known for putting the fear of God into the more timid motorists in the city.

Right: This quartet, who seem quite prepared for any eventualities in the weather, stop to chat near the old Cork Savings Bank on Prince's Street.

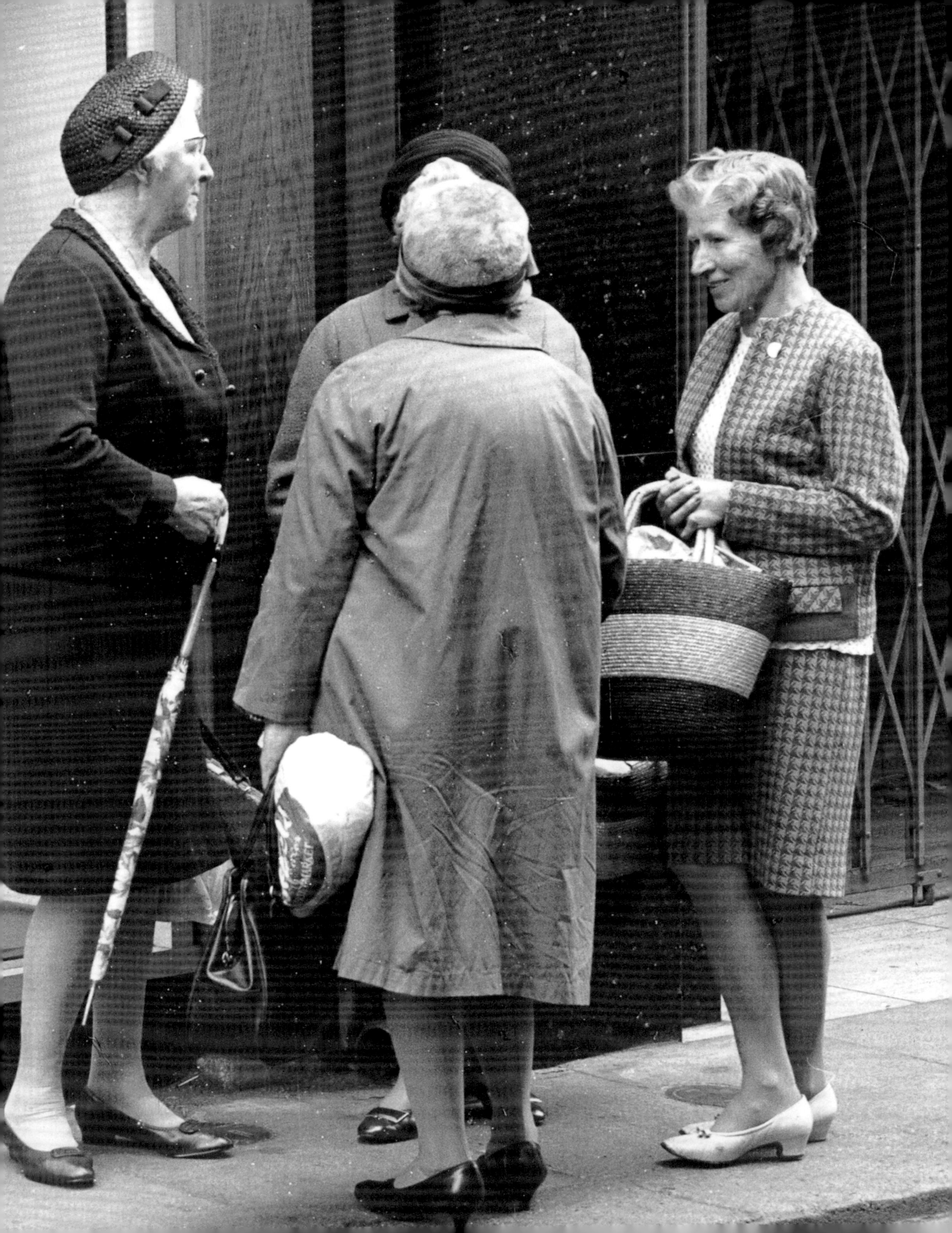

There's a busy day ahead for these dealers on Kyle Street as the pavements are strewn with clothes of all descriptions. If their wares were not sold they had to be gathered up and brought all the way home, so a good selling pitch was essential. The Kyle Street dealer with the cigarette in her hand, talking animatedly, is Maisie Carroll. The woman to the right wearing the headscarf and watching the proceedings is Maisie Hurley.

Reading the *Daily Mirror,* and a more studious book reader, outside the Pavilion cinema in a more leisurely time. The Pavilion cinema opened on Thursday 10 March 1921 and had a seating capacity of 800.

Stella's Coffee Room, on Prince's Street, advertises morning coffee, sandwiches and soup. A man passes the old limestone columns of the Unitarian church next door.

Crossing the road at Dunnes Stores on Patrick's Street wearing that classic Irish combination of sandals and a cardigan.

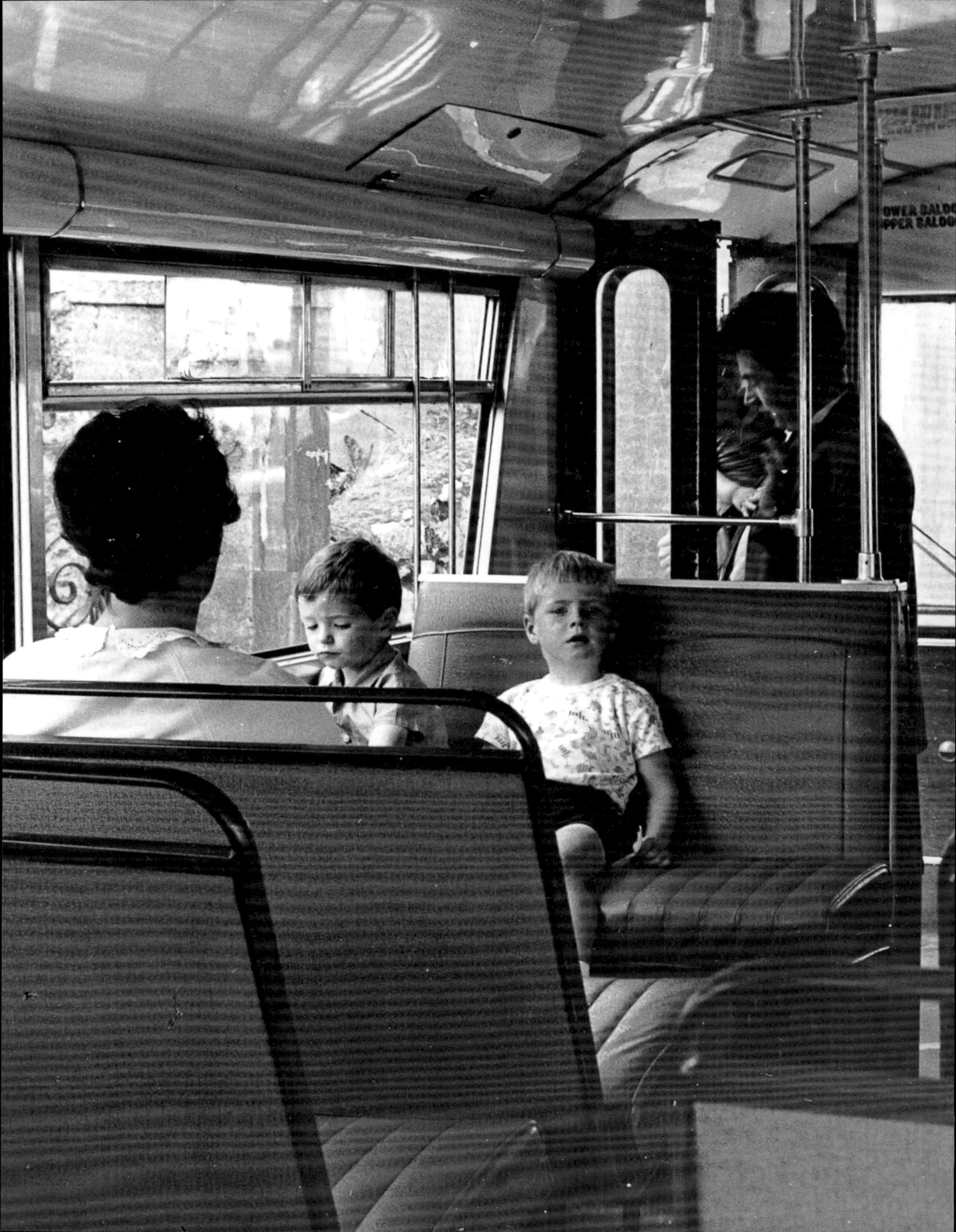

Above: A sign of the times, as a woman in ski pants gives her friends a lift in her mini, parked on Patrick's Street. To the right are the old firms of Mockler's furs and Elvery's sports shop – Elvery's trademark was a giant elephant above their premises. Marie O'Sullivan is pushing the buggy to the right of the picture.

Left: Getting the bus to town was always an exciting time. The old Leyland buses were open at the back with a chrome pole to hold onto when the bus was almost full to capacity.

A nun, dressed in one of the old austere habits, stops near a street lamp as a single-decker tour bus passes on the Grand Parade. In the background is an Austin A40 and just visible is the steeple of St Nicholas's church.

Fashionable haircuts are visible as these women concentrate on getting to the other side of the street safely. The boy watching the stop button is wearing his first communion outfit and badge.

White gloves at the ready, directing traffic near the Gas Consumers Co. store at the top of Patrick's Street.

Elaine Falvey passes the time by sucking her thumb as her little brother Rory holds on to the window sill of this shop on Gerald Griffin street. The eclectic window display includes Drummer firelighters, Odlum's oatmeal, Clover cooked meat, Robinsons lemon barley, Batchelors baked beans, Farley's rusks and, of course, a sign for pigs' heads. The lady standing in the doorway is their mother, Breda.

Three men repairing the roadway outside W. & M. Joyce's confectionary shop (established 1926) on George's Quay. A bag of the best Portland cement stands near the old wooden cart and wheelbarrow.

Shoppers on the lookout for a bus outside Saxone Shoes. A little boy plays with his toy oblivious to the impatience of the queuers.

Above: Two women check out the merchandise on two different stalls, as another haggles with the Coal Quay stallholder before a deal is reached.

Right: Legs folded, bag in hand, this woman rests outside an unprepossessing local licensed premises which advertises Murphy stout. Murphy's brewery was established in 1856.

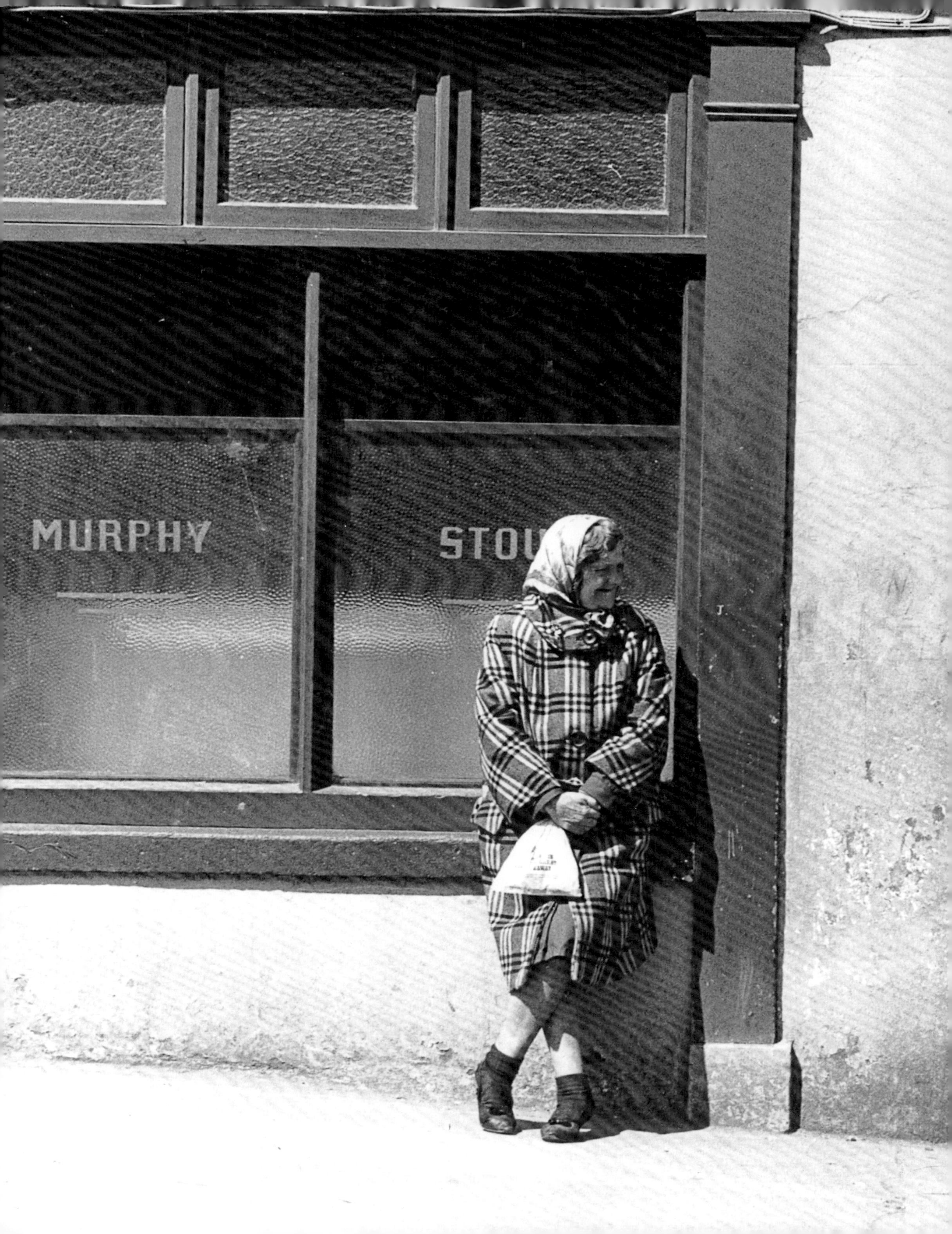
MURPHY
STOU

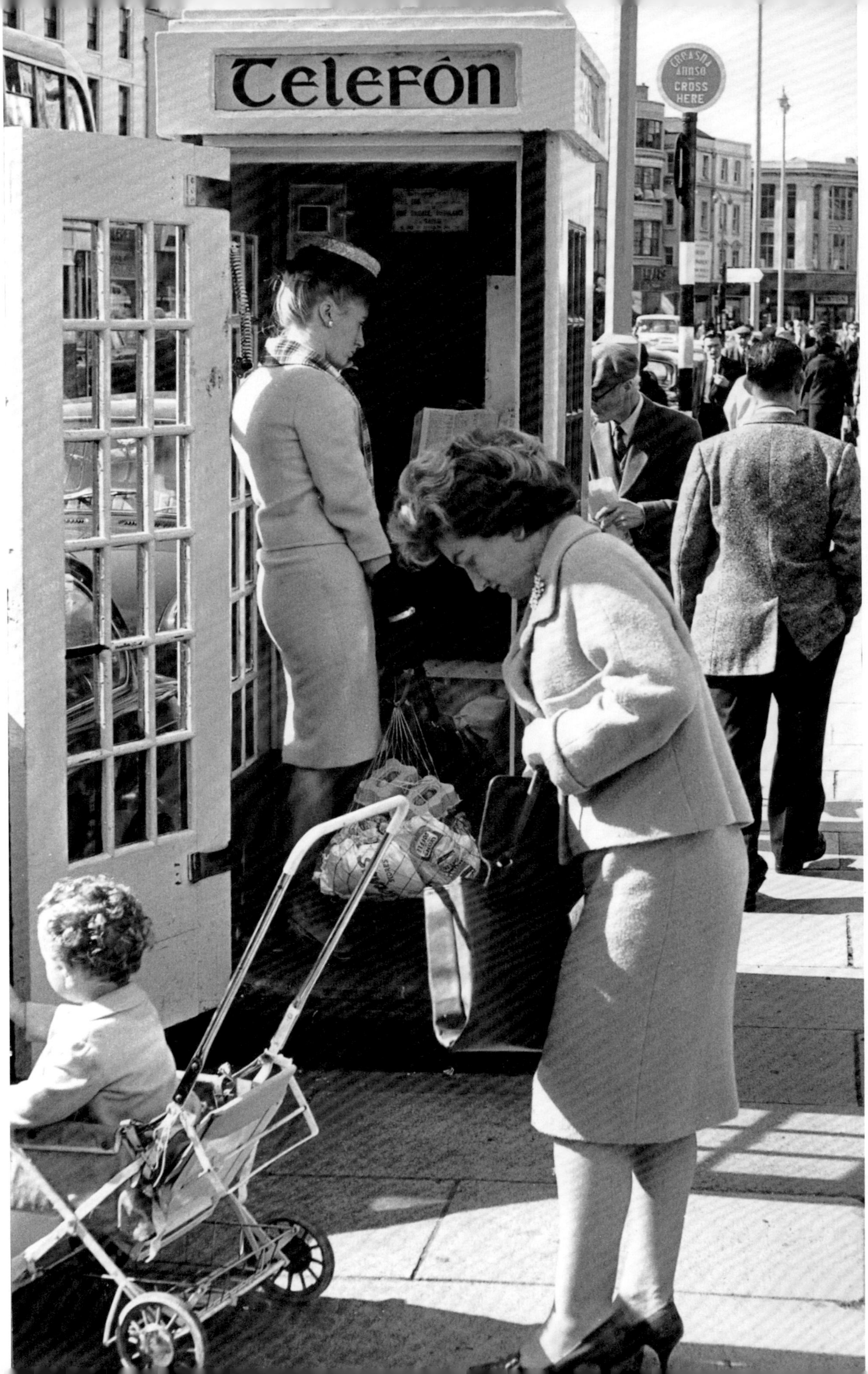
Telefón
CROSS
HERE

Left: The glamorous woman in the phone box sports the very latest Aer Lingus uniform – their premises was across the road at 38 Patrick's Street.

Below: Chatting in front of posters advertising the best in modern music – the Tremeloes, Greenbeats and the Chessmen – playing in Cork. Special gigs were held on various nights in the legendary Stardust Club. Thin Lizzy, U2 and British band The Sweet played there in the 1970s.

Above: A uniformed postman gives directions to these lost souls.

Right: Two Cork shawlies in the market. Christmas trees are for sale in the background as good-natured trader Nellie Roche sells clothes from her stall.

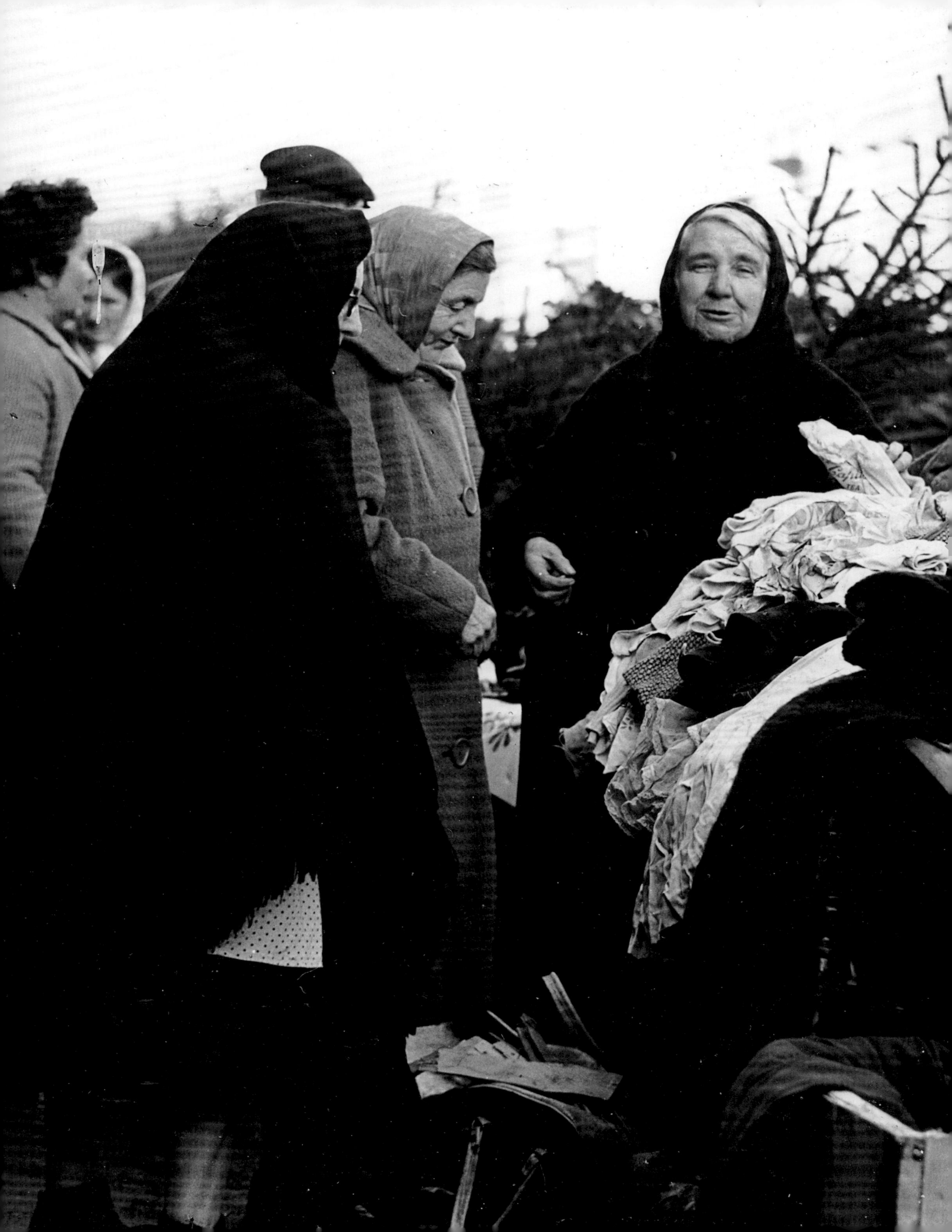

A very busy summertime market on the Coal Quay, with a table full of buckets, shovels and toys on display for the younger customers. The woman sitting on the table selling her wares is another member of the Punch family, Rita.

An unusual visitor to the port of Cork. A submarine was a very rare sight at the time in Cork and would attract much attention.

Above: A busy stall as impending customers gather to look at the garments on sale. The art in selling was to draw a crowd and set the price high so that haggling could begin and customers would compete with each other.

Right: A men's tailors' window with a wonderful display of ready-made suits in the latest fashions and colours. This trend displaced traditional made-to-measure tailoring businesses.

ready tailored
with that
made to measure look
SALE
SUMMER
SALE
TWO PIECE SUITS
READY TO WEAR
FROM
£8.15.0
READY
BURTON
BUDGET
PLAN
EXAMPLE

Above: This man sits on top of a delivery of angle iron which is being conveyed by tractor through Camden Quay. CIÉ were the first to introduce tractors to replace horses in the city.

Right: A carpenter standing in a doorway checking measurements amidst old timbers which were to be reused.

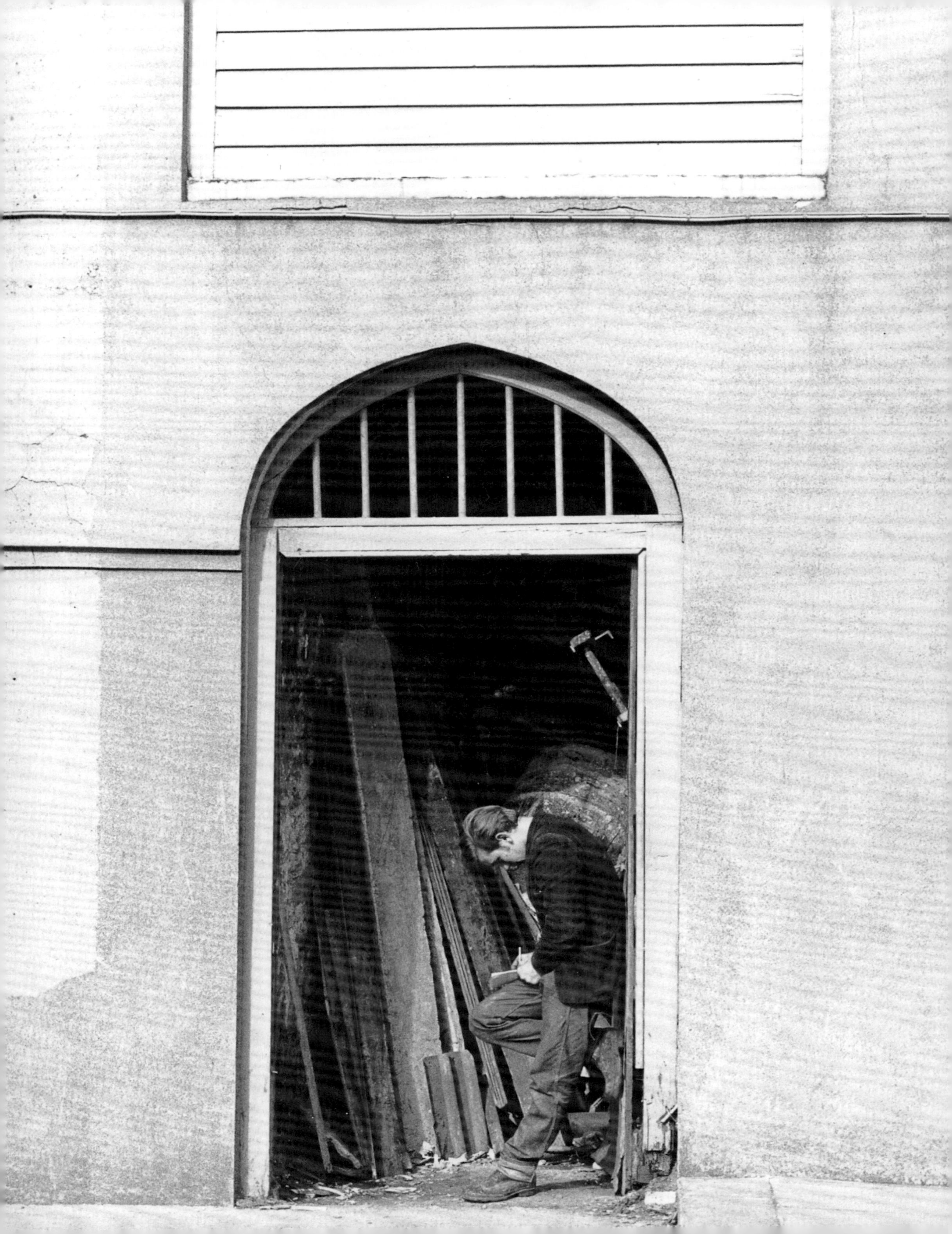

Above: George O'Donovan, the jovial man on crutches, stands next to Mrs Annie Punch outside her shop on the Coal Quay. For many years George owned a chip shop next door, which later became O'Mahony Bros wholesale potato merchants.

Right: This Coal Quay trader, Chrissie Quilligan, wears a duffle coat to keep her warm as distinct from the more traditional shawl.

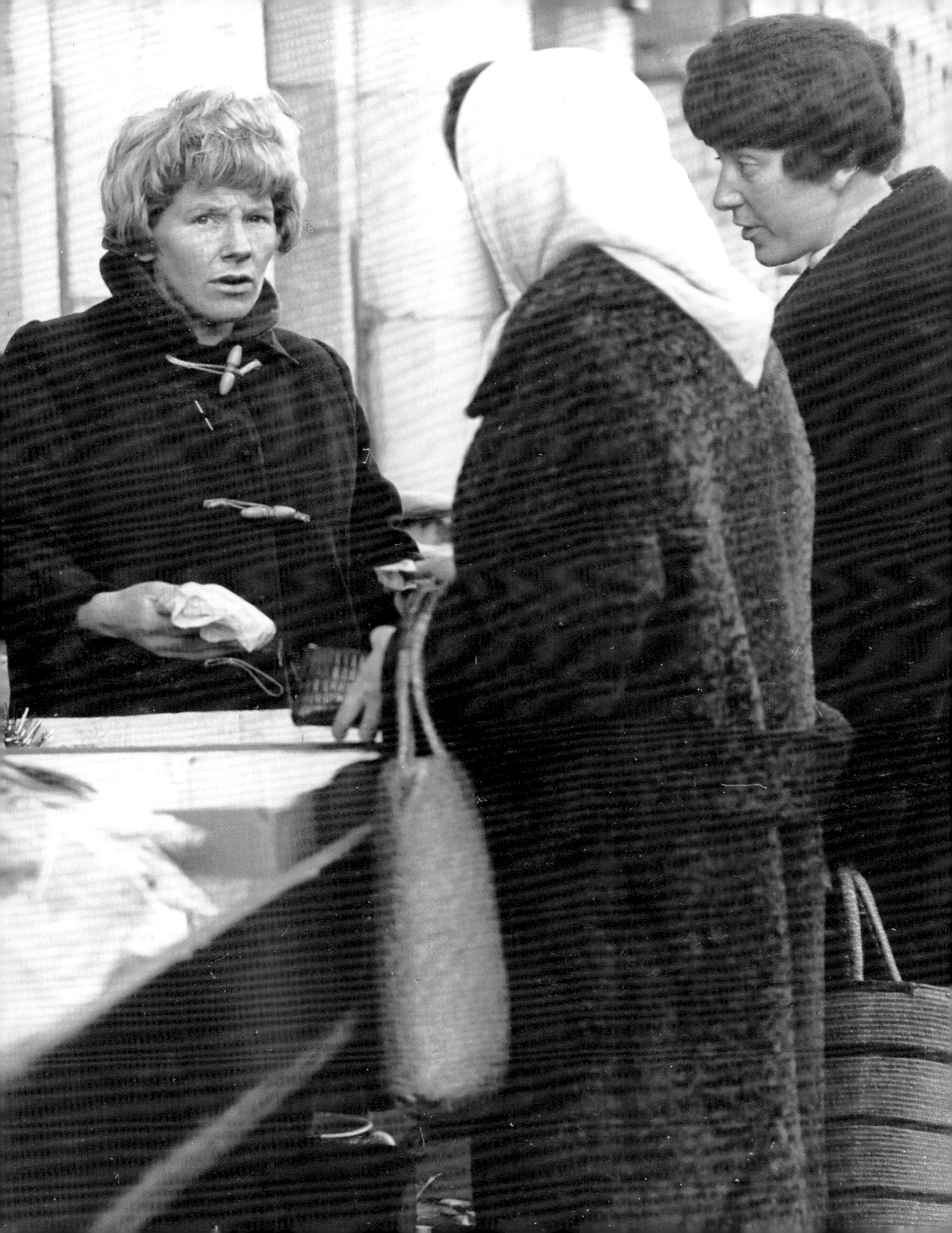

Francis Brennan's jewellery shop at 83 Patrick's Street was located next door to the Pavilion cinema. It was established as early as 1880 and was clearly popular for window-shopping.

Two members of a fishing trawler amidst the fishing nets and motorised winch. During bad weather many of these vessels used to retreat to a safe mooring on the city's quays until the weather changed for the better.

This little girl in her plaid skirt is minding the baby in the pram outside a dry cleaners at the top of Patrick's Street.

A man reads his paper near one of the Wimpy restaurant and takeaways on Patrick's Street.

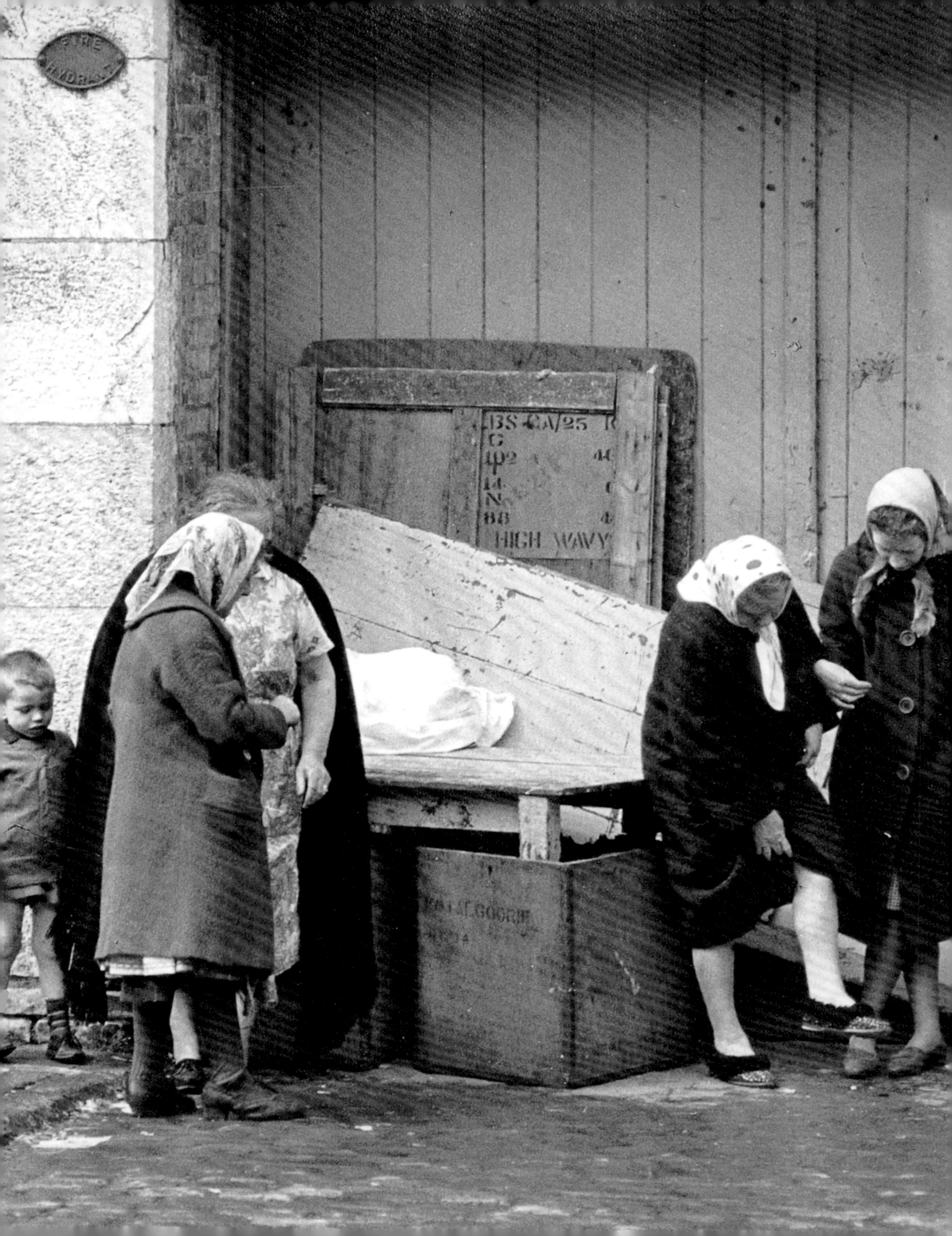
FIRE HYDRANT
BS CA/25
HIGH WAVY

Above: Heading towards the entrance to Clayton Love wholesalers. They specialised in exporting herring, mackerel, shellfish and lobster, both fresh and quick-frozen. They were also a wholesale fruit, grocery and ships' stores provision merchants.

Left: A dealer hides her day's takings down one of her stockings as her companion concludes the last deal of the day. The ramshackle stall would be left overnight near the doorway so that it could be quickly set up again the following morning.

Above: Outside Foley Woollam insurance brokers, 117 Patrick's Street, as the No. 2 bus to Gurranabraher and Churchfield is quickly being filled with passengers and their shopping bags. India tyres are being advertised with the slogan 'Near-things are further away with India Autoway Tyres'.

Right: This man has come prepared with his folding stool as he walks through one of the entrances to the Cork Summer Show.

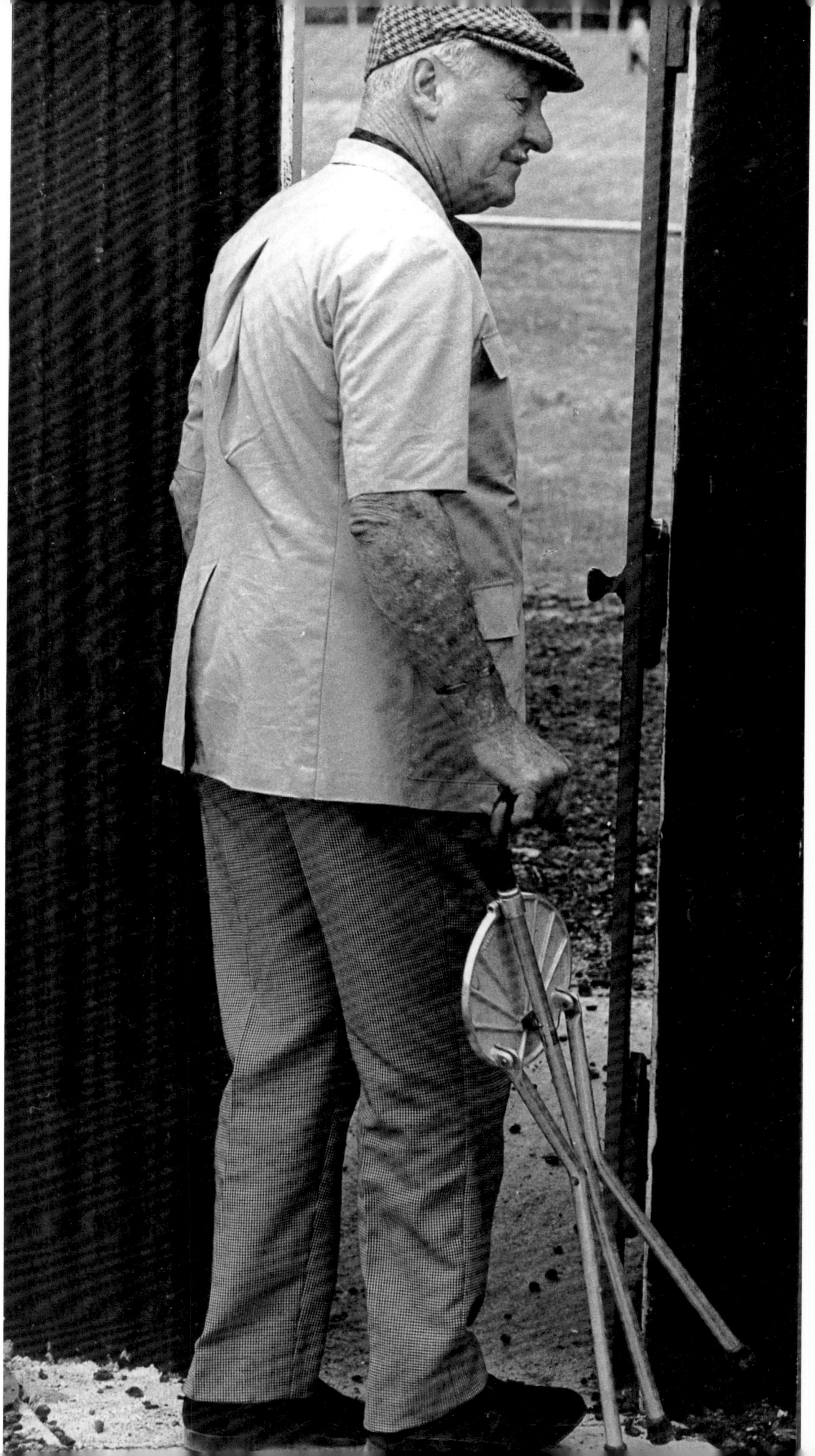

The curved shopfront of Woodford Bourne's provides a wonderful backdrop to these two shoppers on the Grand Parade. Woodford Bourne was once the most specialist wine and spirit store in Cork.

The *Killarney,* which for many years brought day trippers down the harbour, and tug boats were a familiar scene on this section of the quayside at Lapp's Quay.

Above: Christy Dunne playing solo, without his brother Mick, outside Dunnes Stores. The duo were a familiar sight outside Roches Stores and the Savoy.

Right: Conflicting signage says no left turn despite the sign to the Methodist church on Patrick's Street pointing in that direction – hopefully this did not dissuade worshippers!

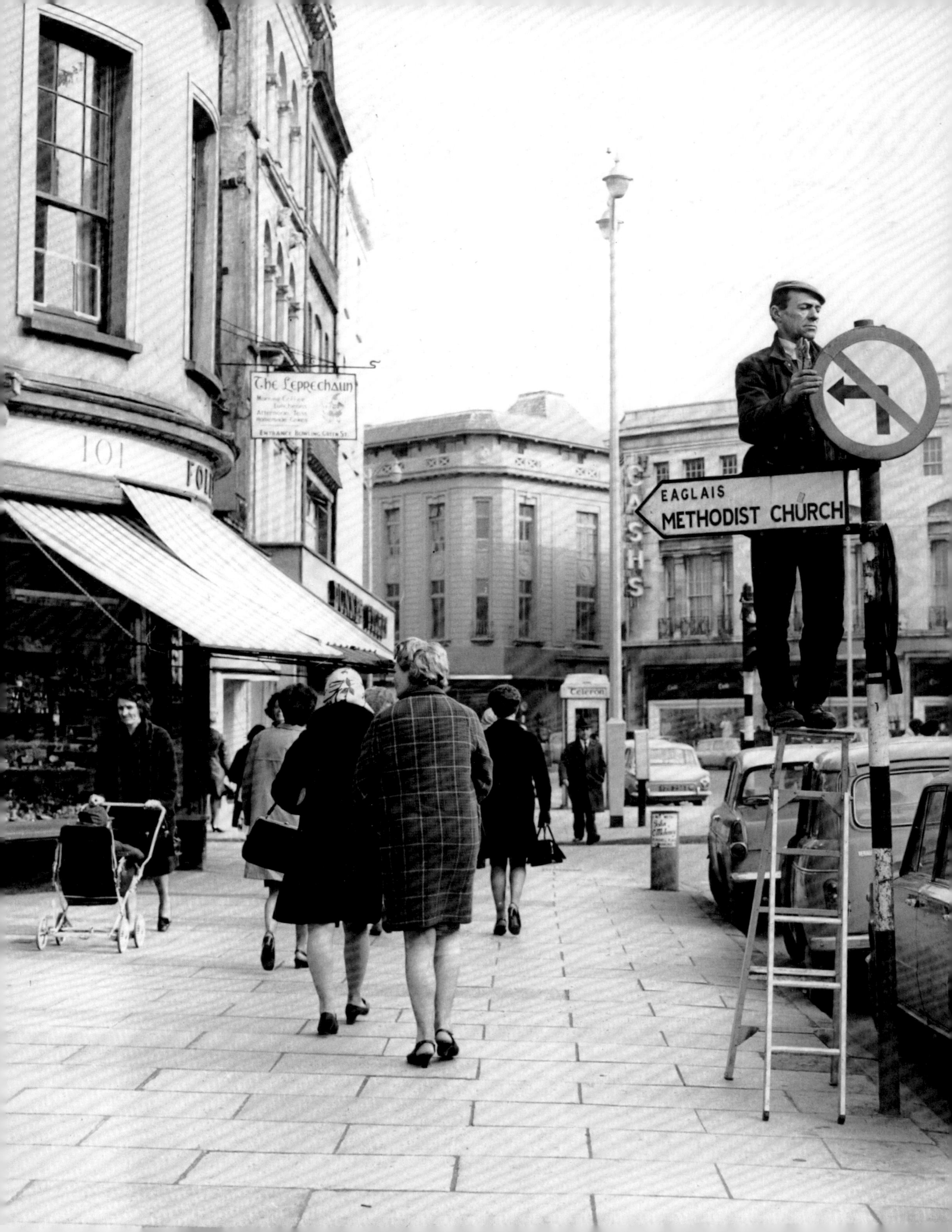

The Leprechaun
101
CASHS
EAGLAIS
METHODIST CHURCH

Above: Various shoppers, including a nun, select from goods in Eason's customer-friendly open shop front.

Below: The Munster and Leinster bank is getting a facelift thanks to the painter with his ladder placed precariously next to the scaffold.

Overleaf: The jewel in Cork's architectural crown, the French Gothic cathedral of St Fin Barre's designed by William Burges, provides the perfect backdrop for Cork's oldest bridge, the South Gate Bridge, which was constructed in 1713.

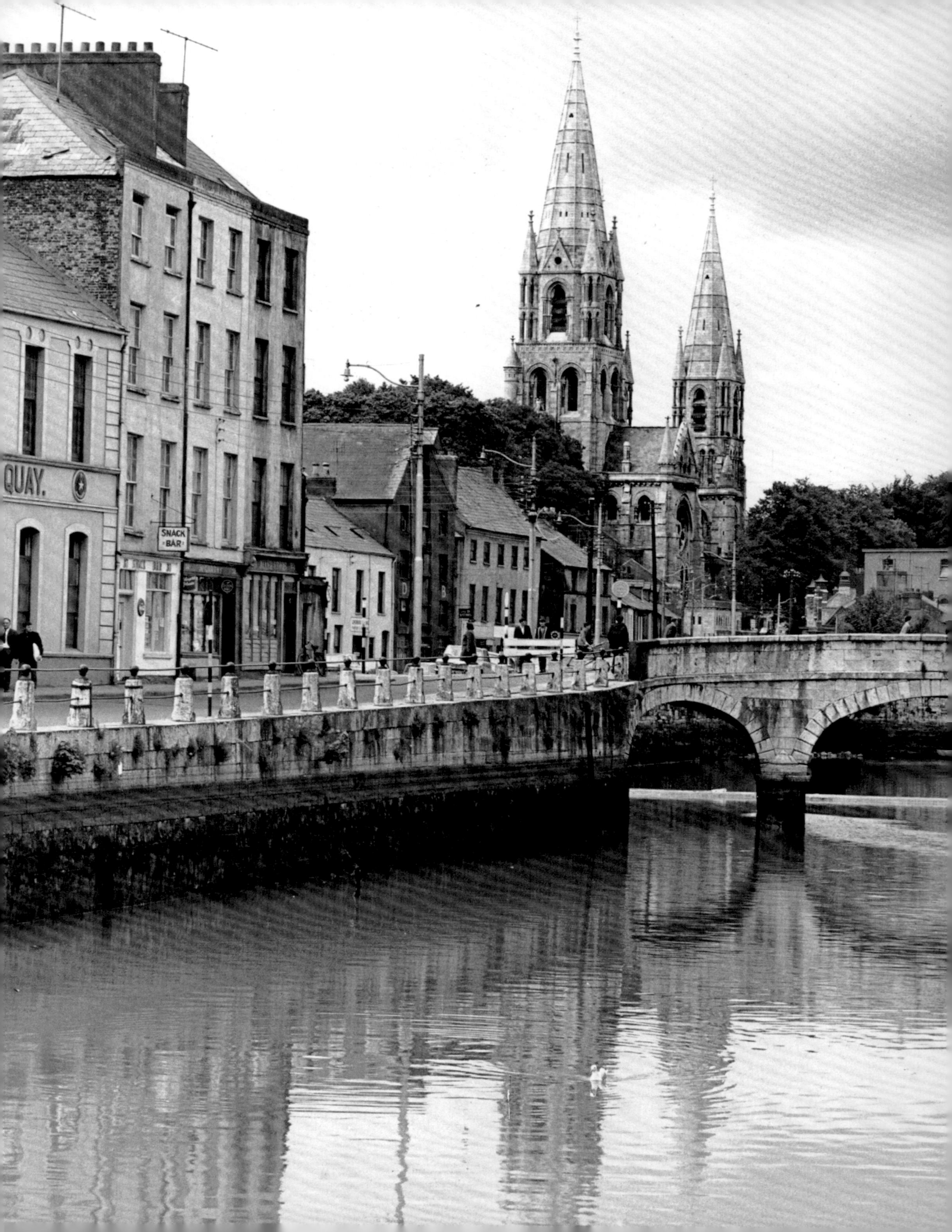
QUAY.
SNACK BAR

Above: The busman's hut on Patrick's Street – CIÉ bus drivers and conductors gathered here for generations. To the left is the Old Bridge Restaurant and another Cork favourite, Clancy's Swan and Cygnet pub.

Below: The old city car park and garage on the Grand Parade. A wonderful array of classic cars are parked near the old P&T telephone box. These include a Volkswagen Variant, Ford Anglia, Austin 1100 and a Rover P100.

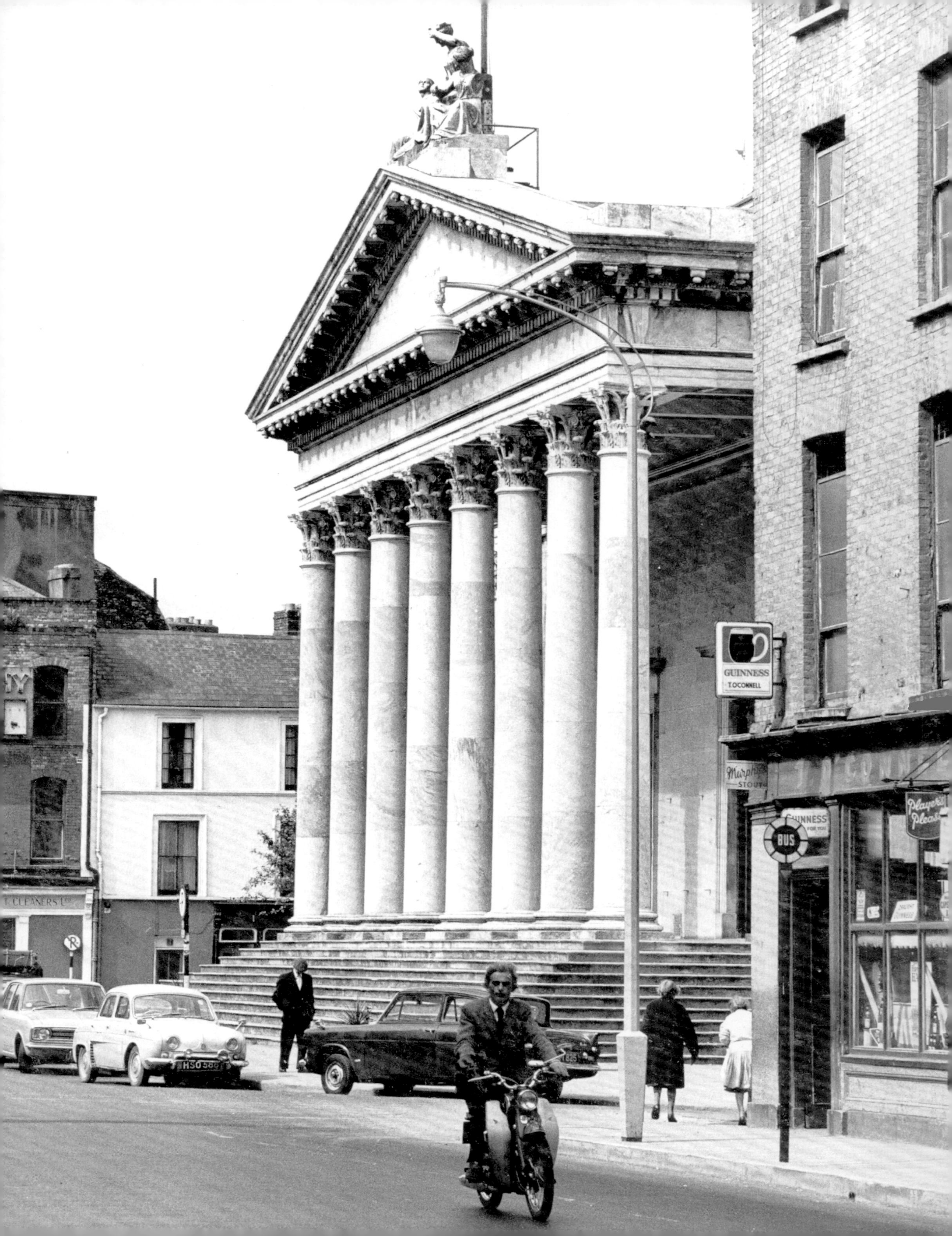
GUINNESS
T.O'CONNELL
GUINNESS
BUS

Above: No traffic jams on this quiet shopping day on Patrick's Street. A garda stands talking to a man alongside a Ford Cortina Mark I. The Ever Ready vehicle parked across the road is a Commer van, in front of the van is an Opel Record estate, and the taxi parked at the end of the street is a Ford Consul.

Left: A man on his Honda 50 drives down Washington Street at a time when helmets were not compulsory, past the wonderful façade of the courthouse, whose Corinthian columns survived the fire of Good Friday 1891. O'Connell's, a Murphy's brewery house, still continues as a licensed premises today under the name the Washington Inn.

ACKNOWLEDGEMENTS

Orla Kelly would like to thank Adelaide Nic Charthaigh, Blaise Smith, Peter Barry, Jacques Restaurant and Barry's Tea.

Michael Lenihan would like to thank the following for their help in identifying subjects in the photographs:
    Denis Lenihan for identifying and sharing his knowledge of the wonderful transport of 1960s Cork.
    Kathleen Barry, Francis Caulfield, Mary Joyce, Ita Murray, Grace Murray, Michael O'Donovan, Barry Punch, Pat Punch, Tommy Twomey and Tony Long for sharing their memories and their help in naming some of the wonderful characters and dealers who traded on Kyle Street and the Coal Quay at a time when it was very much part of Cork's culture and heritage.